Changing
Course

Changing Course

Windcall and the Art of Renewal

Susan Wells

with Seven Profiles
by Sally Lehrman

Heyday Books · Berkeley, California

Library of Congress Cataloging-in-Publication Data
  Wells, Susan.
  Changing course : Windcall and the art of renewal / Susan Wells ; with seven profiles by Sally Lehrman.
    p. cm.
  ISBN 978-1-59714-071-3 (pbk. : alk. paper)
  1. Nonprofit organizations—United States. 2. Spiritual retreat centers—United States. 3. Social reformers—United States. 4. Social action—United States. 5. Windcall Resident Program (Bozeman, Mont.) I. Lehrman. Sally. II. Title.
HN55.W45 2007
303.48'409786662—dc22   2007018227

Photo credits
Chapter 4 (porch and rockers): Joannie Chang, 2005
Chapter 6 (pond reflection), Chapter 9 (wildflowers): Lora Jo Foo, 2000
Profile and author portraits: George Wells
Cover photo and remaining photos: Susan Wells

Design and typesetting:
BookMatters, Berkeley

Printing and binding:
Thomson-Shore, Dexter, MI

Printed in the United States of America

Orders, inquiries, and correspondence should be addressed to:

Heyday Books
P. O. Box 9145
Berkeley, CA 94709
(510) 549-3564
Fax (510) 549-1889
www.heydaybooks.com

10 9 8 7 6 5 4 3 2 1

For Albie
my partner, my teacher, and my love
for over half a century

Contents

Acknowledgments

As I wrote this book I was blessed with the assistance, encouragement, and friendship of Sally Lehman, who, whenever I faltered, used her considerable interviewing skills to help me rediscover the story I wanted to tell.

I am also grateful for the generosity and support of Richard Todd, who affirmed the value of our tale and gently but insistenty pushed me to tell it in my own voice.

Special thanks go to Mac Legerton, who first urged us to record and share what we were learning, and to Betty Medsger, who offered important advice and help at the start of this writing adventure.

Friends Ed Lewis and Mike Clark read early drafts as did three past Windcall residents—Linda Burnham, Emily Goldfarb, and Julia Quiroz-Martinez. Each provided invaluable feedback.

Kristen Wells offered her belief in me whenever my own dimmed and, on one long drive across parts of Idaho and most of Nevada, checked the emotional honesty of my writing as only a daughter could.

Lastly, I want to express my gratitude to the fourteen individuals who, over the years, served on the Windcall selection committee. Their commitment and guidance were essential to the program's success. One of them, Leah Brumer, was both central to the birthing of the resident program and to each of its sixteen years of operation. I am thankful for her vision, wisdom, and cherished friendship.

Foreword

Windcall is aptly named. The word captures the whimsy and the promise of a breeze that plays across the landscape yet contains the transformative power, the hope, and the promise of renewal that is inherent in a building storm.

Sitting here in the drought-stricken Northern Rockies, we think a lot about storms. We need the rain. We need the snow. We need the promise of blooms that follow the storms of winter and early spring.

There are other storms that are caused by human beings, such as the social movements that have transformed America over the past one hundred years. Sitting on my desk is a small black-and-white photograph of Martin Luther King, Jr. and Ralph Abernathy that I took as a college student during the final day of the Selma-Montgomery civil rights march in 1965. For me it is a place marker for the sixties, a truly stormy time during which we saw the birth of so many social movements in this country that dealt with civil rights and racism, war, poverty, feminism, and sexism. These movements were built around the concept of a pluralistic, democratic society that provides adequate space for individual expression, self-determination, and social, economic, and environmental justice.

If these social movements are storms that move across the human landscape, then Windcall is a safe haven, a heart and soul clinic, a personal refuge where people can find nourishment, shelter, and precious quiet time to reflect on what they have learned in the past and what lies ahead in a tumultuous lifelong journey.

Social movements do not come about by accident. They are a crucial, organic response by citizens in a democracy who seek to make their voices heard in new ways. In order for them to be effective, they require a major investment of human and social capital by thousands of individuals who give of their time, energy, and financial resources in order to achieve broad goals for the improvement of society. And they have been effective: Americans have organized political structures to bring about nonviolent social change that would have seemed incomprehensible one hundred years ago.

Nonprofit groups in America now serve as the key means of mitigating the social and economic pressures that have torn apart other societies. They take on the challenges that government and private corporations find too difficult or too complex to resolve. They may also keep us from a second civil war as our society becomes increasingly fractured and as the gap between rich and poor continues to grow at an astounding rate.

For the leaders of these social movements, their successes have come at a high price. Many are so caught up in the demanding struggle for survival of their groups and causes that they compromise their own health and well-being. How is it possible for these people to maintain a balance between their own personal needs, their career goals, and the overwhelming demands of their deeply stressed, underfunded, and overcommitted organizations? How can governing boards of such groups provide ways for their leaders to refresh themselves so that our society does not lose their accumulated experience, expertise, and wisdom? How can those of us who work as staff or board members of such groups ensure that we are applying the same humane management practices to our groups that we seek to achieve for the larger society?

The Windcall Resident Program was created to help social change leaders deal with these dilemmas. *Changing Course* draws on sixteen years of experience and provides valuable insights into the lives and needs of organizers and activists who have chosen to work for social change in America.

I've watched the idea of Windcall evolve over many years. I first met Albert Wells twenty-five years ago, while I was the director of The Highlander Center, a training school for activists in the South and Appalachia dealing with issues such as civil rights and racism, poverty and the environment. He came to Highlander to study the grassroots leadership training programs we were conducting. In the years since, Albert has been a leader on the board of many different social change organizations, two of which I directed: the Northern Lights Institute and the Greater Yellowstone Coalition. During that time Albert and Susan continually searched for creative ways to advance social change. In 1989 they decided to experiment with a program that directly supported individual leaders. They hoped to both acknowledge the dedication of these people and renew their strength. The Windcall Resident Program was the result. With its inception, the Wellses created a tool that has transformed the lives of hundreds of activists. Their efforts beg to be repeated by other people who have similar values, residential facilities, and personal will.

As a lifelong activist I've faced the same pressures as the leaders who have been recruited for Windcall — too little time to meet all of our personal and professional expectations, too little money to meet organizational needs, and a lack of a safe place where one can step back from the overwhelming daily pressures and achieve a long and balanced view of the struggles that define our work and our lives.

Myles Horton, the founder of Highlander and my mentor and teacher, was a leader who believed that our personal experience provided the key to dealing with such dilemmas. When confronted by students who wanted quick answers to unsolvable dilemmas, Myles often quoted a line in a poem by the Spanish poet Antonio Machado, "We make the road by walking." He was wise enough to know that what these social change leaders really wanted was not a simplistic answer but the reassurance that their struggle was valid and that they had a right and a responsibility to keep asking difficult, sometimes dangerous, questions about the unreasonableness of modern society.

What is a reasonable path at a time when our society seems so chaotic and the future so uncertain? Windcall asks organizers to build a personal path that takes their own needs into account. It suggests that leaders of social change organizations have a right and a reason to take care of themselves. For many activists, this may be an uncomfortable idea to embrace at a time when many of us feel overwhelmed by the sweeping forces that seem intent on reducing America to a shadow of what it could and should be. But self-sacrifice is not a viable solution. It does not build democracy, nor does it effectively fight totalitarian leaders and ideas.

The struggle for social change in America is a long one. It is not won by any single victory or destroyed by any single lost battle. We do make the road by walking. The lessons of Windcall suggest that we must make a fundamental change in the way we nourish and support our leaders. We must promote a healthier way to work that respects their need for renewal and reflection. Only then will we provide our movements with leaders who can not only make the road by walking but will make it broader, more humane, more sustainable, and more capable of encompassing a truly just and equitable America.

Mike Clark
Bozeman, Montana, March 2005

Mike Clark is a former executive director, Highlander Center; president, Friends of the Earth; chariman, Greenpeace USA; and executive director, Greater Yellowstone Coalition.

Introduction

Recently, I read about a growing shortage of family doctors in this country. The day-to-day realities facing these physicians have all but erased the satisfactions that led them to choose their careers, said the article in *U.S. News and World Report*. To earn a good living, the average practitioner must keep a few thousand patients on his or her rolls and conclude each office visit in approximately seventeen minutes.

The doctors in the article said that they had chosen primary care because they prized the opportunity to minister to each family not only with their medical knowledge, but with the added expertise that comes from familiarity. Now, they could barely get to know the people who sought their help. During an appointment they might gather sufficient information to diagnose the problem at hand, but they seldom had time for anything else. They had little chance to discuss preventative measures — a healthy diet, appropriate exercise, and regular screenings for skin cancer — let alone probe for signs of addiction or domestic violence. These important conversations couldn't be crammed into an efficient, cost-effective time slot.

The physicians lacked the time to build trusting relationships with their patients and knew that this loss weakened their ability to offer quality treatment. One said that the emotional payoffs of his job had been replaced by "a creeping sense of burnout."

The doctors' laments struck me because for some time now I have been immersed in learning about burnout as it affects another group of people: those who work in poor and low-income communities for social, economic, and environmental justice. They have devoted their working lives to linking the poor and disenfranchised to the rights guaranteed by our Constitution. To do this they must first understand the needs, concerns, and cultural perspectives of the people whom they want to assist. Only then can they begin to teach individuals to become advocates for themselves and their communities. Like family doctors, the men and women who choose a career in this field must invest in building relationships if they are to be effective. Their work is time-consuming and arduous, and many organizers and activists also find themselves on the verge of burnout.

Since 1990, for two months in the summer and again in the fall, the guesthouse of our Montana home has sheltered some of these organizers and activists. More than four hundred individuals of many ethnicities and a wide range of ages have come from all over the United States to take part in the Windcall Resident Program.

My husband, Albert, and I began the project as an experimental response to the large number of leaders in the social change field who, physically and emotionally exhausted from their work, were leaving their jobs prematurely. We were concerned about the loss of their experience and wisdom to the organizations they led and to the cause of social change in general. Since we greatly valued these men and women and the crucial role they played in our society, we hoped to preempt their costly exodus by providing what for them was the rarest of commodities — significant time away from responsibilities and expectations in a beautiful natural environment. We wanted to help them rest and renew their physical and emotional energies before burnout could foreshorten their valuable contributions.

Changing Course tells the story of this sixteen-year project — an adventure that greatly exceeded our original expectations and surprised us with its teachings. As I began this book my objective was to call greater attention to these amazing men and women. Albert and I wanted others to better understand the immense contribution they make to our country. These organizers and activists are committed to making democracy work for all of us — even those who live below the radar of our political leaders' concern. They have long been and will always be our heroes.

As I wrote, though, my goals for the book broadened. In the process of gathering, reflecting on, and recording their story, I began to grasp the motivation and reward that drew this marvelously diverse group of people to work in the social change field. I also saw the personal price they had to pay to pursue their objectives in today's society.

The people you will meet on these pages have made a strong personal commitment to a life's work that is rooted in their deepest moral values. They respect and come to the aid of those left behind by our society. They honor the larger human relationship that connects us to one another. In return, they find greater meaning in their own lives. But our society does not give them the support and recognition they deserve.

In the United States we shower our athletes, film stars, and successful business leaders with ongoing press coverage, adoration, and enormous fortune. Yet we often fail to appreciate those others in our country who express a very different set of values — who heal, teach, and empower people to prosper. We fail to understand the nature of this kind of effort and what sustains it.

It is no wonder that burnout is an ongoing problem in their ranks. Over time the residents have provided us with vital data about the causes and course of this destructive process and directed us, as well, toward effective measures of intervention. At Windcall, we gradually developed a successful model for nurturing and restoring those who work for positive social change. Our experience may offer equally useful information for people in other fields who work from similar values.

We all know and are touched by individuals in our cities and towns who are committed to improving the lives of their fellow human beings. We have moments when we do the same thing. We sit with a friend as he undergoes his first chemotherapy session. We take dinner to exhausted strangers who have spent all day moving in across the street. Each of us experiences moments of recognizing and acting from our shared humanity. At some deep level, we know that response lies at the heart of what our lives are all about.

Increasingly, I thought about how many of the residents' discoveries held meaning for us all. These are troubled times and it is difficult to keep our balance in the face of so much uncertainty and turmoil. In *Changing Course* the residents give moving and candid expression to what can renew the human spirit.

I struggled for almost six months thinking about the best way to tell this story. Our experiment was so full of discovery for so many and yet it was essentially very intimate. Finally I decided to set the reader down at Windcall and let you learn as we all did. I wanted you to see the land because it was such a pervasive force in the process of renewal. I wanted you to hear the residents' voices in prose and poetry as they wrote about their new experiences and re-gathered forgotten parts of themselves. And I wanted you to come along with my husband and me as one of the richest adventures of our lives unfolded.

Susan Wells

Changing
Course

1 Beginnings

May 17, 2004

*t*he bright yellow glacier lilies are the first to arrive. Each star-shaped bloom hangs from its slender, curved stem, face turned down toward the earth. Small clumps of deep purple violets come next, along with a tiny white flower that has at least four look-alikes in the wildflower book.

It is thirty-four degrees this morning and the sky is clear. Our chocolate lab, Jesse, and I are out walking before the sun has made it over the snow-topped Bridger Mountains, and I am grateful for my wool gloves and cap. In one day, the aspens below the studio barn have turned all frilly with tiny, new, yellow-green leaves. Farther down, near the creek, the chokecherries and red-twigged dogwood have lost their sleek winter shapes to a few precocious leaf clusters.

I know that despite the chill in the air, the May sun will have done its job by lunchtime, and it will be warm enough for us to sit on the porch. With enough patience, we could watch the grass grow at this time of year. Spring comes late to Montana, but once started, it comes in a rush.

There are other harbingers of the season. We've started checking off items on our to-do lists. Yesterday Albert turned on the water and heat in the guest-house while I pulled up window shades that have been closed all winter. Over the next fourteen days, while at least two dozen more kinds of wildflowers appear, we will take stock of bedding, towels, and kitchen equipment, clean up the three mountain bikes, get out the gas grill and the porch furniture, and, in general, ready the guesthouse for occupancy.

While robins are busily building their nests in the outdoor lights of the studio barn, Albert will move the potting wheel into place, carry in two new fifty-pound blocks of clay, and get the computers in working order. I will sort the art and writing-room supplies and make a list of missing items to pick up in town. Ted will get the trail horses in shape while he keeps a watchful eye on his brood mares, who should be dropping their foals any time now. And on the last day of preparation, Kay will arrive, her green Honda hatchback full of groceries destined for the guesthouse kitchen.

This is the fifteenth year that we have gone through our spring ritual preparing for the Windcall Resident Program. The first time, in 1990, we excitedly put the finishing touches on the guesthouse and took a deep breath. Then we waited expectantly to see how our experiment would actually work.

Albert and I had no inkling of the adventure that was beginning. Over the years we would meet more than four hundred people who share a profound dedication to improving the lives of those in our society who are denied equal rights and opportunity. These people would teach us about what fuels their incredible commitment. They would also educate us about the personal cost of their work and what they need in order to stay healthy and effective for the long haul. Most importantly, they would deepen our understanding about how to work from the heart in a healthy way and what it takes to heal and renew the human spirit.

It seems strange to us now that we actually backed into this project. Some years before, Albert and I searched hard for a place where we could escape from the busy pace of our San Francisco Bay Area lives. We wanted a piece of land to tend quietly while we sorted out the whole idea of retirement. We chose Montana because for many years it had been a favorite family camping destination. We loved the mountains and especially the four distinct seasons that we had not experienced since we left the East Coast for California.

For two years we visited dozens of ranches, fishing camps, and farms all over the state. Most were too big, too expensive, too hard to reach, or too much in disrepair. In 1985 on a solo trip to check out some land that a farmer had just decided to sell, Albert walked around the property and headed straight for a phone. He called me at home and told me, "I found it."

"It" was a 430-acre parcel north of Bozeman, Montana. Nestled in a protective curve of mountains, the gently rolling land was bordered on two sides by a mixture of aspens, firs, and lodgepole pines. To the west the property sloped in open fields toward a broad, fertile valley. It was a half-hour drive from the town and twenty minutes from the airport, yet situated in such a way that it seemed private and remote. The only standing structure on the land was a grand but badly neglected old barn.

During the next three years we restored the barn and constructed our house and a guesthouse for visiting family members. We also began the process of returning the once-cultivated fields to native grasses. And in acknowledgment of the variety of breezes, gusts, and gales that could softly stir the wind chime, bend the aspen, or howl through the pines, we named our new Montana home Windcall.

As we settled in, Albert began to explore a dream that he thought might fit perfectly into our big barn. In keeping with his lifelong interest in social justice, he began to look into the possibility of running a conference center that would serve progressive causes in the region.

My own dreams, however, had nothing to do with sharing this wonderful place with what I imagined would be a constant flow of talkative strangers. I was too busy appreciating its amazing beauty and stillness and basking in a sense of being deeply nourished. I was savoring the idea of our grandchildren growing up with this land to roam on.

So I was not really upset when Albert came and told me that the conference center project had proved to be too ambitious. He, however, was disheartened. The depth of his disappointment both surprised and touched me. I decided to see if there was another way to honor the essence of his dream but on a scale that wouldn't overwhelm our resources, this slowed-down lifestyle we were trying to cultivate, or my own need for plenty of time alone. I was facing a dilemma familiar to our thirty-eight years together: finding common ground for an introvert and a dyed-in-the-wool extrovert. Devising something that would fit us both had never been easy.

Albert and I could be poster children for the old adage "opposites attract." To begin with, it would be hard to imagine two more dissimilar family backgrounds. He was born in a small New England town that four generations of Wellses had called home. The town's primary employer was an optical company. It was started by his great-grandfather, George Washington Wells, and led, in succession, by his grandfather Albert and two brothers, then his father, George. My Albert was brought home as a newborn to the same house he was to live in for his entire childhood. He grew up in the midst of a large community of relatives, neighbors, and friends. There were usually some twenty-five Wells family members attending Thanksgiving dinner.

Albert was raised with a strong expectation that he could and should shape his world. He was taught that anyone blessed with more than he needs must be willing to shoulder additional responsibility. When he was only eleven, he was sent off to private schools to begin the kind of education that would prepare him for Harvard and eventually an adult life as an informed and involved public citizen.

Six months after Albert was born and about a thousand miles to the south, I arrived. I was named after the heroine of a romantic novel my mother was reading at the time. By age fourteen, I had slept in one hotel bureau drawer and twelve rented apartments and houses and had attended almost as many different schools. As a result of moving around so much, I had more good friends in the pages of books than in the many neighborhoods we briefly inhabited.

My father had worked for the same employer since he was eighteen. The year I was born, he had just begun a planned rotation through three of the company's branches in preparation for a position in the main office in New York City. By the time we finally got there, my much older half brother and sister were both on their own, and I was eleven years old. World War II had just ended and there was a terrible housing shortage; as a result, our residence hopping continued at an awesome pace for two more years. Then, unbelievably for me, our next three apartments were all in the same school district.

I began the second half of eighth grade and continued until graduation at Bronxville High School, one of the best public schools in the country. Most of its graduates went on to college, and I was one of them. I entered a women's liberal arts college in 1952. Wellesley was only a twenty-minute drive from Harvard University.

Albert and I met when we were freshmen, and our relationship continued off and on for the next three years. Despite our dissimilar backgrounds, we were both socially unsophisticated and felt blessedly comfortable in each other's company. Neither of us yet realized that most of the time our instincts would lead us in opposite directions; if we did notice, we probably found our differences intriguing. And while, over time, we would each become the other's most important teacher, we would also develop a livelier and more challenging relationship than either of us might have ordered.

Back then, I thought he was an earnest, kind, and sweet young man, and I was awed by how comfortably and confidently he navigated in the world. He, in turn, was drawn to my curiosity and honesty and was overjoyed to have a girlfriend who wanted to talk about something other than the next party. Since Albert's happiest college hours were spent playing ice hockey and lacrosse, it also didn't hurt that I, too, loved sports. We became engaged early in our senior year, and two weeks after graduation we were married.

I had held an office job every summer since my junior year in high school and had chosen to get a master's degree in education immediately after college. Even so, as a young woman coming of age in the early fifties, I accepted without question that my life would revolve primarily around my husband and children. I had been raised with no expectation that I could or might want to make a difference in the world beyond my family. Both Albert's influence and the political events unfolding around us were about to change all that.

The first fifteen years of our life together were marked by the national turmoil that surrounded the civil rights movement, the war in Vietnam, and the assassinations of John Kennedy, Martin Luther King, Jr., and Robert Kennedy. Like many of our generation we found it difficult to reconcile these events with the country we loved and thought we knew.

We had grown up during World War II. As a ten-year-old boy, Albert often accompanied his mother to a rooftop in town to look for enemy aircraft. He made a scrapbook containing cutouts of every airplane in existence and could more quickly and correctly identify their shapes than any of the adult spotters. My mother was often away on Red Cross speaking tours urging citizens to donate blood, while at home I spent hours in our elm tree pretending to be an air force pilot or bombardier wreaking havoc on the enemy.

Both Albert and I looked forward to the excitement of periodic blackout drills, saved tinfoil from gum wrappers, and went without chocolate to support our troops. On radio broadcasts, in our newspapers, and on movie screens, Americans were the good guys, and it was our soldiers' bravery and the country's patriotic solidarity that turned the tide against evil. We carried that feeling of pride into our young adulthood.

Then, in the late fifties and the sixties, we were shocked to discover the depth of injustice and violence in our nation. The newspapers carried in succession pictures of black civil rights protestors being attacked by police dogs, napalmed Vietnamese children, and our three murdered national leaders. While I agonized about the kind of world our offspring would inherit, Albert felt an abrupt end to his political innocence and an urgent desire to help get our country back on track. He began to spend less time at the San Francisco real estate investment business he had cofounded when we moved to California in 1960. Instead, he became increasingly involved in social justice issues.

Albert's concern quickly made him a guiding force in Abelard, the small, private, nonprofit foundation that we, with six other Wells family members, had set up in the late 1950s. He also became increasingly involved in the effort to identify and organize national business leaders to voice their strong opposition to the Vietnam War. In addition, he began what would become four decades of service on the boards of various nonprofit organizations that were fighting for social, economic, criminal, or environmental justice across the country.

I was an active board member of Abelard, and I could be found wheeling a stroller in most local peace marches. My primary concern from age twenty-two to thirty-four, however, was raising our three children, Melissa, Kristen, and George. When our youngest was eight, I began to think about pursuing my growing interest in the field of psychology. In typical fashion, I spent a year reading about everything from Freudian psychoanalysis to school guidance counseling. Midway through one book that offered a moving and intimate look into the author's practice of individual psychotherapy, I knew I had found the long-term goal I was after. The writer was Jim Bugental, a clinical psychologist working in nearby Palo Alto, California. I picked up the phone and called him.

That telephone call was the beginning of an amazing experience that would ignite in me a passion as strong as Albert's quest for social justice. I was one of eight people invited to join in the creation and staffing of a nonprofit, low-cost counseling center operating under the licenses, supervision, and incredible generosity of Jim and three colleagues.

In the six months of intensive training that followed, I reveled in weekend workshops and classes led by an array of experienced therapists. As we began our counseling work, we not only saw individual clients, but also co-led several therapy groups with one of the professionals. After five years at the center, I decided to pursue a graduate degree in psychology. I had found a career I loved. It involved what I valued and enjoyed most: individual relationships, education, and healing. Best of all, it challenged and engaged my mind and intuition in equal measure, and it demanded of me all the creativity I could muster.

At forty-one, I opened my private practice. Eventually I also began teaching continuing education courses for younger therapists and supervising their work. Many of the most talented among them, I discovered, struggled with deep fatigue and the unraveling of their private lives. In order to gain the hours of experience necessary for state licensing, most held low-paying jobs in nonprofit halfway houses and community clinics. They always had more to do than they could possibly accomplish. Many also had difficulty setting reasonable limits for themselves because the people they assisted were in such dire need. I found myself teaching my students as much about managing their commitment to their work as about treating their clients.

At the same time, Albert was noticing a high level of wear and tear among the directors and staff members of the many social justice organizations on whose boards he served. The excessive incidence of turnover concerned him. He also heard about organizers and activists struggling with sleeplessness, mood swings, and physical exhaustion. These were classic symptoms of "burnout"— a word coined at about that time to describe the destructive effects of habitual overwork.

Albert and I remarked on the obvious similarities between the young therapists working in direct-service nonprofits and social justice workers doing community organizing. Both groups found their jobs personally rewarding, but work often demanded more time and energy than they could humanly deliver. Even as they sought to help people with complex and serious problems, they had to struggle with organizations that were understaffed and underfunded.

In the spring of 1989 these experiences came back to me to feed the germ of an intriguing idea. Perhaps I knew a way to ease Albert's disappointment at having to abandon his conference-center dream. For assistance in thinking it through, I turned to the executive director of our foundation, Leah Brumer. She had the important qualifications of knowing both of us well and understanding the shared values we pursued through Abelard. One afternoon Leah and I sat for several hours in a coffee shop in Berkeley. I poured out my concerns and wondered aloud about an idea that might replace the center. I remember distinctly that the wooden stools had begun to feel very hard before we were through hatching our plan.

We talked back and forth about how we could fit together the pieces: the land and existing accommodations, Albert's desires and my own needs. Slowly we began to shape a new kind of investment in social change. Through Abelard grants, Albert and I had financially supported progressive organizations and issues for over three decades. Knowing as we did the worrisome incidence of burnout in the field, why shouldn't the two of us provide direct support for individual leaders themselves? Through our foundation work, we already had direct connections to the kind of people we wanted to reach.

Targeting the workers on the front lines of social change, we could invite them to stop, leave work behind, and take what they so rarely had: time for themselves. As our guests at Windcall, they could rest and refill exhausted reserves. In this way we might honor their valuable contribution and strengthen their future efforts. I took our idea home and Albert was delighted.

We had the land and direct access to the adjacent national forest. We had a pond, some well-trained riding horses, and our huge old barn. We had an underused guesthouse. We even had an activist turned cowboy for a ranch manager. The longer we thought about it, the more convinced we became that building a resident program for organizers and activists was an experiment worth trying.

As for the size and duration of each session, that was easy. Our guesthouse had four bedrooms, so we would have four residents at a time. The climate pointed to a two-month session in the spring and another in the fall. The month of August could be reserved for us and for visits from our extended family. We began at once to make a list of possible members for a national selection committee and an advisory board.

We had come to Montana hoping to discover how we wanted to spend our retirement. I had been looking forward to finally exploring a long-held interest in oil painting. Albert had hoped to create many more opportunities for play, while still keeping his hand in social change. Neither of us would have guessed that we were about to begin an experimental project that would become our primary shared focus for the next decade and a half. Nor did we foresee that it would use our differences to maximum advantage and be one of the most satisfying and rewarding adventures of our lives.

2 The Residents

We need to work toward an alternative vision of society that is centered around human dignity, self-determination, and compassion. And, oh yes, this is a life-long journey. In front of my desk is a quote from the Talmud that says, "Look ahead, you are not expected to complete the task, neither are you permitted to lay it down."

—*Helen Kim (1999)*

*t*he people we met through the Abelard Foundation gave Albert and me our first real education about the dedication and passion of those who work for social justice. We made one of our initial grants in the early 1960s to a group that was registering black voters in Mississippi. Recent civil rights legislation had created new opportunities for these citizens, but they needed hands-on assistance as they attempted to exercise their hard-won rights. In some areas, whites were blocking county offices and intimidating would-be voters. Organizers prepared and accompanied these courageous people as they confronted a long-standing racist political system.

We also funded a nonprofit in West Virginia that was organizing coal miners who suffered from black lung disease. These men had spent years laboring in inadequately ventilated mineshafts and many now could barely breathe. In the face of powerful resistance from the company owners, organizers helped these miners demand a healthier work environment and just compensation for those who were disabled.

The people who struggle to advance positive social change have been our personal heroes ever since. They play a role that is both protected by our democracy and crucial to its success. Most of these organizers and activists labor full time to link the disenfranchised to rights and benefits guaranteed by our Constitution and legal system. They empower people to become advocates for themselves and their communities. Others challenge institutional practices that erode social, economic, or environmental justice, leading the search for more equitable solutions.

We created the Windcall Resident Program for these individuals: the people who seek to strengthen our nation and promote the highest values of our participatory system of government.

Our residents have come from all over the United States. They work on behalf of inner-city children, small farmers, exploited workers, and the victims of racial or sexual discrimination. They help communities deal with hazardous waste disposal, the need for low-cost housing, and AIDS education and care. They strive to find solutions to homelessness, inadequate health care, and hate crimes. By wrestling with these issues and many others, they push our society to realize its full potential and promise.

These men and women also reflect the diversity of America. They represent many ethnicities and every level of formal education. They come from large metropolitan centers and small towns. They may be grandparents, individuals in midlife, or young adults. And like the rest of us, they have rent or mortgages to pay, children or elderly parents to take care of, relationships to maintain, and losses to mourn. They are ordinary people, but they take on extraordinary tasks. They do this despite the difficulty and challenge inherent in their work and the personal price their effort often demands.

Our residents have shared with us their various motivations for choosing a career in the field of social change. Some have told us that their choice grew out of events that occurred in their youth. At dinner one night, Katy Heins described how, at nineteen, she joined a group of student volunteers in her Midwestern city to work in a nearby low-income neighborhood. Armed with saws, hammers, and paint buckets, they rehabilitated substandard apartments in a recently established nonprofit housing co-op. Katy also participated in a sit-in at an abandoned building in a successful effort to secure it for addtional homeless housing.

The power of collective action amazed her. She saw the difference that ordinary citizens could make if they joined together with a clear and common goal. A decade later, in the same community, Katy became the director of a grassroots organization that pushes to make county welfare more effective and humane. Most of her staff members are former recipients.

During the summer between two years of graduate studies at Duke Divinity School, Melinda Wiggins worked as an intern with Student Action with Farmworkers (SAF) in North Carolina, assisting migrant Latino agricultural workers with immigration applications and a home ownership project. This experience reconnected Melinda with her own family's agricultural and working-class history in the Mississippi Delta. After graduation Melinda continued her efforts to improve conditions for poor people in rural communities. She became program director and two years later the executive director of SAF.

Although Alex Poeter was born and raised in Germany, he currently runs a multi-issue community-based organization in a low-income neighborhood of Chicago. He still vividly recalls visiting a concentration camp when he was sixteen years old. He stood transfixed and horrified in front of a mound of hundreds of shoes that were worn by children who died there. That unforgettable image, he told us, serves always to motivate and remind him that we all must confront the abuse of power.

For many residents, the decision to work for social justice grew out of first-hand experience similar to the inequities they now strive to correct. An African-American from the South, Rosalyn Peles is the daughter of a factory worker. She has experienced racism, classism, and sexism all too often in her life. These forces have fed her thirty-year commitment to freeing others from similar oppression and injustice. She began her work in the civil rights movement and later went on to anti-Klan organizing. Now her focus is the workplace, especially the concerns of women of color working in low-wage jobs.

Helen Kim's family came to the United States when she was twelve. She cared for her three younger siblings while her parents took second jobs on graveyard shifts to support their family on minimum wage. When she first began to work at the Asian Immigrant Women Advocates (AIWA) in San

Francisco, her brother teasingly referred to her efforts as her "make-up-to-your-mother campaign." Just like the members of AIWA, Helen's mother had been an electronics assembler. She would come home with her eyes burning and her head aching from handling toxic chemicals. Now Helen works to protect other women from those hazards.

When I first saw Clara Luz Navarro, I was struck that her diminutive size and sunny disposition gave no indication of her enormous courage and sense of commitment. For twenty-five years Clara Luz worked as a nurse in community health programs throughout rural areas of her native country, El Salvador. The poverty and health problems she saw there sparked her political and social conscience. She decided to run for mayor in her city and use her campaign to confront the government's failure to help the desperately poor outlying communities.

Clara Luz's outspoken convictions so enraged members of the political establishment that they threatened her life and forced her to flee her country. Even though she had a child, little money and no family support, Clara Luz volunteered as an organizer in her new community within months of finding work in the United States. In her off hours from her jobs — first as a healthcare worker and later as a researcher at UC Berkeley — she worked with a group fighting for temporary protective status for other Salvadorans fleeing persecution. Little by little she learned to trust that here she could express herself freely without threat of torture or death.

Clara Luz went on to found and direct Mujeres Unidas y Activas, a grassroots organization dedicated to developing the self-esteem and collective power of Latina immigrants. She drew heavily on her own experience to prove to other immigrant women that it was not only possible, but within their rights, to engage in organizing and activism in the United States.

Unfortunately these freedoms, which some Americans take for granted, are still and increasingly under fire in some areas of our country. Jaribu Hill directs the Mississippi Workers Center for Human Rights. She has worked with organizers in the Deep South for ten years and knows all too well the slow process of change. Her organization has been assisting newly elected black female mayors and low-wage workers in tiny towns in rural Mississippi. These towns are in the middle of cotton fields and catfish farms, and even though the population is as much as 90 percent black, white plantation owners and their descendants have ruled them since the time of slavery. Jaribu told us that recently some white folks, angered by the election of a black woman as mayor, ransacked a city hall. They took the computers, the law books, everything. Jaribu's organization provided legal help and linked this brave woman to others in the region who are also attempting to shift the balance of power.

It was a specific threat to his rural Maryland community that unexpectedly catapulted Michael Shea into organizing. Michael had his own small construction business and a passion for sailing on nearby Chesapeake Bay. Then, in 1993, he learned about a proposed billion-dollar development of luxury houses that would destroy the last large wetlands near his home. In his application to Windcall he explained:

> Franklin Point is an interwoven ecostructure of ponds, streams, creeks, tidal wetlands, grasses, and marsh. It is the nursery for much of the fish and Atlantic Blue Crab caught in our waters — the fishery that supports our remaining indigenous water people. It's the winter home for our waterfowl — a variety of ducks, Canada geese, and hundreds of tundra swans. There was only one choice for me: organize.

With no previous experience in community action, Michael founded the South Arundal Citizens for Responsible Development. He and his friends wrote and distributed leaflets, thought up edgy slogans for street signs, turned out citizens for public hearings, met with officials, organized demonstrations, and more. They were sued by the developer for libel and would have lost their homes if they had lost the case. But after a five-year battle, they won.

Michael's group ultimately did more than protect the 477-acre wetland. The victory they achieved empowered the entire community. It raised their collective confidence and encouraged them to work together on additional projects that would serve citizen interests.

About seven years earlier in Brooklyn, New York, a different neighborhood felt the reverberations of one person's efforts and resolve to meet a community need. Freddie Hamilton couldn't find any decent local day care and, as a young, single working parent, she desperately needed some. The solution she worked out for herself eventually had a huge effect. She organized other mothers in the neighborhood to create and staff a child-care center. That was the beginning of the Child Development Support Corporation, which Freddie still directs. This organization now serves thousands of African-American and Hispanic children in all five boroughs of New York City and employs more than one hundred and thirty people.

We have learned over the last fifteen years, however, that these powerful accomplishments often carry a high price tag. Even though our residents display a commitment that comes from their very core, their staying power sometimes seems superhuman given the difficulty of their job. Their work rarely is contained to a five-day week, nor are the emotions it engenders. Many toil in communities where people barely make ends meet and where despair is endemic. Every day these residents experience the underbelly of our nation and the suffering that flourishes there. Somehow they must learn to shoulder the stress of this frequent and unavoidable exposure to the pain of others.

Mac Legerton is a tall, gentle man with a soft Southern accent and a love for western swing dancing. In the late 1980s he and his family received threats of violence because of the interracial work he was doing in Robeson County, North Carolina, the most ethnically diverse rural county in the United States, with black, white, American Indian, and Latino citizens. The warnings became even more frightening when a close friend, a Native American candidate for Superior Court judge, was assassinated. In his application to the resident program, Mac wrote that nothing could have prepared him for the terror and trauma he felt. On an intellectual level he knew how difficult the work of social justice could be, but the actual emotional and physical strain stunned him.

People like Mac have a deep compassion for the struggles of other human beings. That compassion can make them vulnerable to moments of anguish. During an investigation of an alleged incident of brutality, a young lawyer with the nonprofit Office of Citizen Complaints in San Francisco was trying to ascertain if a police shooting had been race related. As she uncovered the facts, Diane Chin empathized with both of the two young men involved. Regardless of the outcome of her inquiry, she could not stop imagining the dreadful consequences for both the victim and the accused.

My dreams were of a young man dying, a young man who merged with other men of color in San Francisco who have died in police custody. My dreams were also of a frightened police officer making a split-second decision and realizing that someone was dead because of that decision. I was both men at varying times in my dreams.

Our residents also must contend with the reality that they are fighting entrenched inequities that may have changed little over generations. Not only is the work slow and arduous, but sometimes progress may be fragile, undone by such things as a change of administration in Washington or a downturn in the economy.

That was certainly true for Emily Goldfarb, who struggled for decades to improve immigrant rights in California. In 1994 the state passed laws that drastically unraveled most of the progress she and others had spent years achieving. Even in the midst of mourning lost ground, however, Emily and others like her recognized an essential lasting gain: their work had strengthened immigrant communities by increasing their political savvy and developing leaders who would mount future efforts to regain their rights.

Those who work for environmental justice now face similar setbacks. Conservationists despair as standards for clean air and water are being methodically undermined. They struggle to respond to the current administration's commitment to corporate growth and energy exploration in previously protected wilderness areas. They mourn the cost to the land. They also know that the people who will suffer most from these changes are indigenous and low-income communities, like the Gwich'in Tribe, who inhabit the oil-rich, far northern tundra of Alaska, and those who live in the shadow of Louisiana's high-pollution industrial area — the so-called cancer alley.

Yet the people who come to Windcall and others like them continue to chip away at the intractable ills they find in our country. They do this work because they know they are addressing critical human needs, redressing abuses, and building a stronger, more inclusive society. They also do it because it enables them to truly live their values and to work from their hearts: to use their skills, life experience, and passion to empower and improve the lives of others. As community organizer Joshua Hoyt wrote in his application:

Organizing is not just about issues and victories; it is about deep beliefs, about reflecting, about teaching and mentoring, and about passing values on.

Despite the inevitable hardships and pressures involved in their work, the overwhelming majority of activists and organizers who come to Windcall find it hard to imagine another career that would be as satisfying. They are sustained by their belief that moving the American system ever closer to its highest ideals is the most important goal they could pursue.

I Saw a Mist Overcome a Mountain

Standing in the foothills
I saw a mist overcome a mountain.
Tenuously at first, but the mist persisted.
I saw a cloud conquer the hills
Not from above, but from the hill's breast.

I saw a mist overcome a mountain.
A mist of humble droplets
Weaving themselves together
Seeking valleys, gulches, paths and canyons
Finding, winding and climbing their way through.

I saw a mist overcome a mountain
Determined and united, tiny drops of water
Conquered the mountain in their path.

I saw a mist overcome a mountain.
Tiny drops of water climb a hill.
If a mist can conquer a mountain,
And small drops of water overcome a hill,
Then why not you and I?

—Scott Douglas (2001)

3. The Road to Windcall

*Every day it seemed there was a new pile of papers on my
desk. Campaigns begun, projects unfinished, telephone calls
unanswered, pressures to do this, that, and the other. No
time. I was, to say the least, frazzled. I wouldn't have even
filled out the Windcall application if my assistant at the
Urban Habitat Program hadn't kept putting it on top of
the pile.*

—*Carl Anthony (1992)*

C arl Anthony has a lot of company. Almost all organizers and activists feel
that they have no free time and would clearly understand what Carl
means by "frazzled." Their applications, like his, end up on the bottom of a
never-diminishing pile of papers, but very few get repositioned by a supportive assistant. In fact, it takes potential residents an average of three years to
actually fill out a Windcall application and send it in.

This time lag was not something Albert and I had expected when, with
great excitement, we sent out the first wave of some three thousand brochures
all over the country. If anything, our staff and we feared that we might be
inundated with applications. All of us were stunned when only six people
responded. Here was an opportunity to come to a beautiful setting and enjoy
several weeks of free time, good food, and the company of compatriots — all
expenses paid. We knew how many organizers and activists badly needed
some time off. Why didn't more jump at the chance?

First we considered expanding our outreach efforts. But when we checked with some of our contacts in the field, we discovered that we were reaching plenty of eligible and deserving candidates. Then we rethought the application itself. We had tried to make it simple and friendly. But since we didn't plan to interview our candidates, we wanted more than a statement of their job experience; we asked applicants to write about their personal histories and their visions for social justice.

This request turned out to be part of the problem. Most potential residents simply couldn't carve out the time to sit down and think about what they wanted to say, let alone put it on paper. They kept waiting for a break in the action, which never materialized. Then, after a year or two of conversations with the residents who did show up, we began to identify other important hurdles that stood between applicants and their first step on the road to Windcall.

It certainly didn't help that in our country we value high energy and tangible accomplishment and see the need for leisure as either a character flaw or a symptom of aging. For men and women working in the nonprofit sector, however, there are even more compelling demands to keep going without a break.

In fact, for those who probably most need Windcall, it is a tremendous stretch to even imagine taking time off. Dan Hirsch cofounded an organization that focuses on the safety of nuclear power plants and the accuracy of information available to local communities. His was the first citizen's group to successfully prove a secret partial meltdown at a Department of Energy site and to get the facility shut down. In his application, Dan described the day-to-day pressures inherent in his social justice work.

> The life of many organizers is one of constant crises. We work ungodly hours, at triple pace, under less than comfortable circumstances. We try to put every ounce of smarts into strategy to counter the immense power of our opposition. However, to be successful, given the imbalance of forces, we have to be ten times smarter, ten times faster on our feet, and — and this is the cruncher — willing to work ten times harder.

Nonprofits like Dan's operate on incredibly tight budgets. They face an ongoing struggle to meet the payroll, pay the rent, and fund their programs.

They must constantly raise money. The staff is lean and employees are often on the job evenings and weekends.

Even if potential residents feel that their organizations can survive their absences, each day brings fresh reminders of the backlog of work that would pile up and be waiting when they return. They also know that taking time off will add to the burden of coworkers. It is easy for many to conclude that these consequences outweigh personal needs and that stopping to rest is an indulgence they and their organizations can little afford.

For those who surmount those concerns, tricky personal logistics and emotional complications may still block the path. Some have to call on the generosity of family members or friends to help with the care of a child or an elderly parent. Others may feel guilty about taking time away from partners or children who already see too little of them. For many leaders in the field of social change, taking a break from work hardly seems worth the effort.

Then we came across another deterrent, one that haunts many in the field of social change and compromises both their health and their effectiveness. A damaging nonprofit work ethic still flourishes, one that encourages people to override their own needs in deference to the importance of their task. It holds that truly committed individuals should be willing to tackle the Goliath of social injustice regardless of the personal cost.

This standard of conduct was present and active in Fran Barrett when she considered taking time away from her job. As she began to fill out her application, Fran struggled with embarrassment that she needed a rest. With a growing sense of failure, she wondered if she was just not trying hard enough. A voice inside accused her of being lazy despite her more than twenty-five years as the founder and director of an organization that provides management assistance to approximately 150 nonprofits serving New York City residents affected by poverty.

Kay Whitlock was brought up in a blue-collar town in southern Colorado once known for its steel mill blast furnaces. When she came to Windcall, she had already spent more than thirty years working on issues including farmworker support, women's health, and lesbian, gay, bisexual, and transgender rights. Even some of the most respected organizations she served seemed to expect almost limitless self-sacrifice as a necessary part of the job. She recalled one human rights organization, for instance, that was built on work overload at almost every level. More than a few nonprofits are so focused on getting the job done that they end up creating the very kind of dehumanizing environment that they are struggling to change for others.

Albert and I slowly realized that providing support to these heroes of ours wasn't as simple as offering them rest and renewal; too many found it too hard to make use of the opportunity we were offering. At the same time, we began to see why so many in this field were vulnerable to overwork and the risk of burnout. When it came to tending to their own health and well-being, most of these experienced, capable leaders were rank beginners.

Every group taught us more. It wasn't just the intense demands of their jobs or the culture of the workplace that led applicants to ignore their own needs. By far the most insidious restraint was their own feeling that they didn't really deserve a break. These individuals work every day with people who lack access to such basic things as a roof over their heads, a job, a decent school for their children, and health care. In comparison, their own lives were far easier. Why should they take time for themselves and abandon others who were less fortunate to struggle alone?

When Michael Stoops came to Windcall, he had not had a vacation in twenty-plus years of working in the homeless advocacy movement. He had felt that taking time off was not only an outrageous luxury, but also morally irresponsible. He believed that when homeless people got vacations and could go to a retreat, then he could take care of himself. Michael compared his own needs to those of the people he served and never felt that his were compelling enough to warrant serious attention.

Other residents grappled with concerns for fellow workers whom they judged more deserving and who had overcome much more difficult struggles and still kept working. They ended up burdened with guilt about even considering a rest. Most reached for their application only when exhaustion or poor health shut them down and justified their need.

Many of the organizers and activists who came to Windcall seemed similar to the young therapists with whom I had worked. Although they were adept at assessing and attending to the needs of clients, they seemed slow to notice or respond to their own. At some point while they were growing up, they had acquired a fine talent for taking care of other people, but this was paired with an inability to use that very skill on their own behalf.

Almost all residents also share two attributes that give heart and power to their work. The first is a well-developed sense of personal responsibility toward others. Born and raised in Iowa, Bob Hudek grew up with the idea that he was answerable for events and needs in his larger community. In his application he wrote:

> We all come here as people who are committed at some level to the idea that the world can be a better place and that we will accept responsibility to act in a powerful way to make it better.

Bob codirects Wisconsin's leading public interest organization. Wisconsin Citizen Action works to ensure statewide affordable health care, quality education, and comprehensive campaign finance reform. He and his wife, Kate, had a foster child in addition to their three other children. Bob considers himself an optimist, but he also finds constant reminders of the injustice in the world.

> I see the looks that my fourteen-year-old son's African-American friends get when they walk down the street. I know the struggles of my sister-in-law and her partner building their family in a world that thinks that their love as two women is threatening or evil. I have seen the loss of dignity in my father's best friend as she struggles to pay for prescription drugs that cost over half her income.

Our residents all share Bob's sensitivity to the plight of others and keen sense of empathy. They are capable of standing in another's shoes and comprehending that person's experience. This ability guides their organizing strategies. It also undergirds their commitment to empower those who are marginalized in our society.

Dan Hirsch goes further in explaining the important role of empathy. He says an emotional understanding of human oppression creates the urgency and drive that fuel any organizer's work.

The suffering in the world can be mitigated or stopped only by
the extraordinary efforts of those who feel the lash on another's
back as though it were on their own, and who in fact understand
that it is.

As I met more residents like Dan and Bob in Windcall's early years, I
began to understand more clearly why so many qualified people were having
trouble accepting the Windcall invitation. As with my young therapists, the
very qualities that give enormous strength to social justice workers also carry
a potential liability. While they might be skilled at assessing human needs in
the external world, most have blocks when it comes to their own well-being.
Similarly, while they are quick to respond to others with compassion, many
find it difficult to extend such understanding to themselves. They are not
good at setting reasonable limits on their work and making time for their own
healing and renewal. Instead, they are likely to accept self-sacrifice as an
inherent part of their commitment.

I wager that this profile is common to many of us who work in professions
focused on addressing the needs and supporting the struggles of others. I think
particularly of teachers and nurses. Their ability to suspend their own boundaries and enter another's reality is a natural gift that early life experiences and
years of practice hone into a well-developed capacity for empathy. Unfortunately, this valuable talent has a flip side that we need to recognize and rem-
edy: a tendency to assign less importance to self-care.

With each new resident, our understanding of the individuals we were
trying to serve increased. At forty-five, Elena Herrada is a single mother of four
daughters and a grandmother of a one-year-old boy. She also has an adopted
daughter from El Salvador whom she brought to the United States for a long
series of burn surgeries. Elena has spent most of her adult life living and
organizing in the working-class communities of Detroit, a city she claims is
"not for the faint of heart." She assists people with survival issues: how to feed
their families and pay for rent and child care. In telling us how her job had
impeded her journey to Windcall, she mentioned another powerful consequence of keeping up with the demands of her work.

Getting away from my quicksand life in Detroit to come here was one of the hardest things I've ever done. Working-class urban industrial life is merciless and operates at an unrelenting pace and clamor. If I was not aware of the constant strain in my life, it was because I had disconnected my senses — unplugged my humanity — in order to get through the day and keep pressing on.

Elena coped by shutting herself down and silencing her feelings. She was able to keep going only by ignoring the internal signals that would have reminded her of the personal price she was paying. That numbing made a simple decision to apply for a residency almost impossible. She was restrained by both the needs of others and her own survival mechanisms.

Many of us can identify with this way of dealing with too much pressure. From time to time all of us can temporarily go on automatic in order to push ourselves beyond our limits. We deny signals of exhaustion; we even ignore the constraints of actual time. And while we may initially succeed in keeping up the illusion of progress, reality eventually brings us to a grinding halt: we catch a cold, double-book appointments, or get so grouchy that family members complain.

When individuals face work characterized by unrelenting pressure, the tactics they use to withstand that pressure may shut out all physical awareness of the harm being caused. Contemplating this, we began to see how burnout could easily take root in the ranks of organizers and activists. We sensed how they might unconsciously harbor its seeds within themselves and inadvertently feed its growth. Our vision of the resident program's purpose began to expand. Perhaps Windcall could be more than a rest stop for activists and organizers. Perhaps we should shape a more specific response to their susceptibility to habitual overwork. But first, we would need to use our newfound knowledge to help more residents get here.

While we didn't necessarily have to throw our outreach net any wider, we did need to haul it in with increased care, precision, and perseverance. Our potential residents required more support and encouragement than we had imagined. The staff began to make personal follow-up calls to likely applicants. Then we asked our supporters and past residents to stay in touch with those they referred to Windcall and push them along. In their feedback to us, newcomers stressed the effectiveness of being "hand carried," especially when the hands were those of fellow organizers or activists who reassured them that their organizations would be in fine shape when they returned, and so would they.

We also learned that potential residents break out of some of the numbness Elena wrote about by just beginning to answer the questions on their applications. As they take time to reflect, they begin to notice the symptoms of overwork, though they may not label them as such. Some register with surprise how long they have been in the struggle and how tired they are. Others begin to recognize that work has been so central to their lives that disentangling themselves becomes not only a logistical problem but an emotional one as well.

Much to our surprise, some individuals ended their applications with expressions of gratitude for what they had gained from filling them out. They added that even if they were not accepted to the program, they had received a valuable gift. Many who went on to be residents told us later that writing the personal essay was the start of their Windcall education. Thinking about and recording their history and vision was a powerful interruption of business as usual and made their first step on the road to Windcall an inward one. With their second step, they would begin to discover what exactly lay at the end of that road.

Perhaps the message here at Windcall is this: maps not needed for this trip. All that is needed is a clear and open heart and mind and a supportive community.

—Bruce Plenk (1992)

Work

I don't want to work hard anymore.
I want to work soft.
I read about soft energy today
The resources of sun, wind and water.
I read of hard energy—
Of fossil fuels and splitting atoms
Consuming resources and returning poison.

I don't want to work hard anymore.
I want to work soft.

How did this happen?
What makes me work this way?

Perhaps it is the Puritan ethic
The industrial revolution as God
That says I'm worthless unless I worry as I work
And produce something tangible
Some proof of my value and purpose.

Or maybe it's because I feel such
An utter sense of responsibility
That I must always do one more thing
Before I rest.
Then another,
Then another.

I don't want to work hard anymore.
I need to work soft.

—*Mac Legerton (1990)*

4 Settling In

The first night here was strange. I didn't know what to do, so
I walked down to the big barn alone and watched a movie.
After it ended at one AM, I turned it off, opened the door and
saw nothing but the silhouettes of mountains and a dark gray
sky. The wind was so loud and the guesthouse seemed so far
away. I tried to walk calmly at first, but then, feeling my heart
race faster, I started to run back like mad.

—Regina Botterill (2001)

*i*t is only when new residents ascend the final hill to Windcall that they begin to realize how far beyond their familiar environment they have really strayed. Lying on the southern edge of a small valley that cuts into the surrounding Bridger Mountains, the ranch is bounded on its east and south sides by the Gallatin National Forest. For about a mile to the north, pastures and grain fields pattern the land before it rises to soaring peaks. To the west, the Gallatin Valley stretches for forty miles before being contained by the Tobacco Root Range.

Since few residents have ever seen the Northern Rockies, the setting stuns them: the sheer mass of nearby mountains, the breadth of sky, the panoramic view. Some find the landscape as disturbing as it is magnificent, particularly those who live and work in low-income urban centers. They are used to street-lights and the all-night glow of the city, the steady hum of densely populated neighborhoods and the sharp sounds of traffic and voices. As Ilana Berger, a community organizer from Brooklyn, put it: "Silence in my neighborhood is when the car alarm stops so you can hear the people yelling outside."

At first, for people like Ilana, the darkness of Windcall nights and the silence — broken only by the sounds of nature — are unnerving.

The residents' abrupt dislocation is not only geographical. They have also traveled far from families, friends, and coworkers. Many feel uneasy and cautious. A few even seriously question their decision to spend several weeks with a bunch of complete strangers and whatever other creatures might inhabit the acres of the ranch. Luckily, most newcomers quickly discover that despite the grand and expansive surroundings, Windcall is a sheltered and sheltering place.

From the very beginning of the program, our goal was to create an environment that supported a carefree, restful existence. We wanted our residents' temporary home to be serene and snug, a place for privacy and quiet moments but one that also encouraged conversation and interaction between its four inhabitants. We wanted the guesthouse to feel luxurious but not seem like a place that needed careful use.

To this end, Albert and I installed a variety of well-seasoned, comfortable furniture, grouping soft couches around an excellent woodstove that was efficient and easy to use. We hung a colorful variety of paintings and posters on the walls and added a few bright scatter rugs. Then we filled the rooms with some of our favorite things.

Any month in Montana might bring weather that makes me want to linger inside with a good book. So I put plenty of pillows on the residents' beds and living room couches and boosted the latters' appeal with a few woolly throws. Then I crowded the bookcases with an assortment of novels, mysteries, and nonfiction adventures. I also added a stack of challenging jigsaw puzzles and games and stocked the kitchen with such bad-weather essentials as locally roasted coffee beans, teas, hot chocolate, and popcorn. Last, but far from least, I placed a large cookie jar in a position of prominence on the kitchen counter.

Albert made sure that there was a working flashlight in each closet, assorted sizes of bad-weather gear on a coatrack downstairs, and a large selection of rubber mud boots and umbrellas near the back door.

For good weather we put deck chairs and wooden rockers on the porch and a rope hammock in the front yard. Albert stuffed a basket with contour maps and trail guides, and I stowed daypacks and water bottles in the hall closet. We hung a couple of broken-in straw hats and baseball caps just inside the back door and placed two well-used mountain bikes outside.

The bikes come in handy for special excursions, but walking is the primary mode of transportation at Windcall. The main buildings on the ranch — the big barn, the studio barn, and the home of the ranch manager, Ted Bryan — are no more than a five-minute stroll down the road from the guesthouse. Uphill and within shouting distance is our home. This close proximity encourages a natural and easy sense of community.

We all cross paths, quite literally. We walk the same trails, leave our dinner tables to watch the same sunset, or call between houses to tell of a bear or elk sighting. Occasionally we share a conversation, a walk, or a meal. I help with the horseback rides, Albert fixes the guesthouse sink that clogs on a fairly regular basis, and Ted brings the mail on his way back from town or stops by to invite residents to ride or to watch a horse shoeing.

The Windcall staff very quickly loses its stranger status, starting right at the airport. Nancy Stetter waits for arrivals at the designated meeting place beside a twelve-foot-tall bronze bear in the main lobby. After the bear the first thing residents are likely to notice is Nancy's smile. It crinkles her whole face and somehow permeates her voice as well. Most newcomers already know that voice. From the moment they were accepted to the program, she has been their Montana phone contact, always ready to help with travel plans, answer questions about climate and clothing, and address any special concerns they may have.

Only about one-third of our residents drive their own cars to Montana, so Nancy makes a lot of trips to the airport. Every other weekend in June, July, September, and October, she piles newcomers and their suitcases into her station wagon and takes them to the ranch. Since she has lived almost all of her sixty-one years in this region, Nancy has considerable knowledge of the area that she eagerly shares en route. In her younger days, she and her husband ran a dude ranch in Wyoming. Now she has her own personal coaching and consulting business.

Those residents who come by car are also likely to be met upon their arrival. Erica Harrold drove here from the West Coast, where she is political director of California Peace Action. She was greeted by the most exuberant member of our welcoming committee.

> Jesse, the Wellses' chocolate lab, was the first being I met at Windcall. I'd pulled into the driveway unsure where to go, in awe of the beauty, and wondering if anyone was even around. He was silently watching me. I caught his eye and we did that momentary animal instinct thing—friend or foe? I smiled sheepishly and he returned it with one of those heart-melting dog smiles and ran down the hill to welcome me.

Jesse is an important companion for many of our residents. They call him their borrowed pet and claim that he is a great hiking guide as well. Many are certain that he will protect them with his life from meaner beasts in the woods—although luckily their assumptions have never been tested. Albert and I are sure that Jesse believes the resident program exists to provide him with a constant supply of dedicated walkers and hikers. We do nothing to dissuade him.

Whether greeted by human or canine, each group of residents comes together for the first time to share the evening meal. Dinner also brings the cook.

Kay Rasch is in her early sixties. She is a wife, mother, and grandmother. On first meeting she appears shy and reserved, although a true observer couldn't miss the spark of ready humor in her eyes. One bite of dinner leaves no doubt about her love and talent for cooking, but it may take longer for residents to discover that her second passion is for dancing of all kinds. Kay has worked for us as head cook since 1992. She and a variety of weekend assistants have handled the various dietary restrictions and preferences of our residents with good humor, imagination, and mouth-watering success.

Residents are likely to get their first glimpse of Albert and me on the day following their arrival. The year the program opened, we scheduled an introduction and orientation meeting for their first night. We were so enthusiastic to meet each group that it took us a few sessions to register the glazed look in many of their eyes. We did not yet understand the depth of exhaustion they brought with them, nor did we add up the weariness resulting from travel and time changes. Finally, we got the picture.

Perhaps it came after one remarkable resident disappeared into his room upon arrival, closed his door, and slept for three days straight. His feat might have been even more impressive had his fellow residents not called us to come and make sure that he was still breathing. With some apprehension, we knocked on his bedroom door and he appeared — groggy but smiling. Soon after that we hung a blackboard in the guesthouse hall and wrote our welcome, adding a note that we would come down the next afternoon to greet residents in person. Even so, an occasional new arrival will show the disheveled signs of having been hastily awakened just in time for our appearance.

The focus of our orientation has changed a lot over the years, too. At first we talked primarily about logistics: meals, housekeeping, mail, telephone messages, and the like, as well as available activities, such as hiking and riding. We were anxious to get out of the residents' way and leave them to enjoy every minute of their stay. Then, as we got wiser about the level of anxiety some experienced being in Montana, our emphasis changed to include matters of personal security.

When various hate groups and Western militias were in the national news, we reassured our guests about the safety of our immediate neighborhood. Aware that residents of color might feel especially uneasy, we also relayed reports from previous residents about the respectful treatment they had received in the predominantly white city of Bozeman.

We've also learned to teach our residents about how to behave with our various livestock, occasional hunters in the forest, Montana's incredibly fickle weather, and anything else that might seem threatening. We spend a lot of time on native animals — especially black bears. We instruct residents in the use of bear spray and urge them to carry it while hiking in our woods. Albert is quick to admit that in eighteen years he has only used it once, and there wasn't a bear in sight. He was attempting to discourage a particularly persistent skunk from building a winter nest for his family under our front porch.

After we finish our talk, Albert brings out maps of the region with Wind-call clearly marked on them. Then he piles everyone into the van and drives them around so they can get physically oriented to the boundaries of the ranch and where it sits in relation to other points of interest. He sprinkles his narrative with generous bits of the lore, legend, and history of the region. He also throws in some local gossip about movie stars generated when several scenes from *A River Runs through It* and *The Horse Whisperer* were filmed in our valley.

The following day, everyone's vision of a genuine cowboy knocks at the guesthouse door. Ted Bryan is slender and soft-spoken. His ever-present cow-boy hat shades intense blue eyes and an impressive handlebar mustache. When he introduces himself, it is impossible to imagine that he was born and raised in Maine. Nor would anyone suspect that he went to an Eastern prep school and spent the spring of 1972 in the streets of Washington, D.C., protesting the war in Vietnam.

Ted left college and came west when he was twenty. It was then that he earned his cowboy credentials. For eight years he lived and worked as a cow-hand on a ranch within the Northern Cheyenne Reservation. Ted has been the Windcall ranch manager since we purchased the property and has been a major part of the resident program from its inception. He plans, teaches, and leads all horseback riding. He also invites residents to the weekly neighborhood yoga class he organized years ago, which meets every Tuesday morning in the big barn.

Past residents also add to the intimacy at Windcall through the writings they leave behind. Our first year, we asked everybody to leave a message for those who would follow. We suggested that they record impressions about their experience and offer any tips and guidance they wanted to pass along. We also photographed each group and collected their pictures in albums for the guesthouse. As new residents explore these albums and writings, they feel their sense of dislocation ease.

Before Marcy Whitebook left Windcall, she wrote about the hours she spent immersed in those books. Marcy's passion has been to make high-qual-ity child care available to working parents. At the same time, she has sought to increase the wages, benefits, and status of this traditional women's occupation. One night Marcy couldn't sleep, so she scooped up all the Windcall photo albums and the three-ring binders holding the written *Impressions*. She spread them out on her bed and matched individual stories to pictures until two in the morning.

> You know, if you flip through those photos, you realize we all look pretty similar. The grinning group at the guesthouse and the duded-up crew with the horses. But our stories — whew! When I climbed in bed with all those people what I rediscovered was a multitude of voices, each person experiencing Windcall in a different way, each telling a different story about how this place has affected them.

The thick volumes hold surprisingly candid accounts of the trials, joys, and discoveries of past residents. These writings, like our staff, bring comfort and encouragement. Residents find in this collection of messages an intimate reminder that others share their values, struggles, and commitment. While they sometimes offer contradictory advice such as "don't miss the Leaf and Bean coffee shop in town" and "never leave the ranch," together the *Impressions* suggest that all newcomers find their own best use of Windcall and honor that.

There is, as well, another kind of affirmation that helps residents settle in. Albert and I discovered it quite by accident. One day we started our welcome by telling the group that they were sitting in our guesthouse because we held each one of them in high regard. We told them that we deeply valued the work they had done and that we understood the personal sacrifices they often made. We said we were grateful for their dedication and courage and that the resident program was our way to thank them.

No one spoke. As the silence deepened, Albert and I grew increasingly uncomfortable and nervously launched into our more practiced script about daily logistics. Then a resident interrupted and told us tearfully that even though her organization and its projects had received recognition, this was the first time she could remember being personally thanked. Nor did she recall anyone ever acknowledging the necessary sacrifices and long hours that were part of her commitment. We were embarrassed to realize that we had never before thought to speak our sentiments out loud, even though they were the foundation of the program. Since that awakening we include similar words in each orientation and many other residents have echoed that first response.

Kathy Goldman is a plainspoken, no-nonsense New Yorker whose organization supplies meals to thousands of poor people. She wrote to us after she left and posed a question that she had pondered and finally answered for herself.

> It's not as if some of us have never received an accolade of one kind
> or another for our work. Why does this feel so different? It's because
> everything at Windcall is saying to us, "*You* deserve this, you deserve
> the best and here it is."

Albert and I have come to believe that our message of appreciation has such a big impact because we understand and honor not just our residents' accomplishments but their initial choice and continued commitment to do this difficult and valuable work. They pour their whole selves into their jobs and often pass up more prestigious and lucrative employment in order to do so. And we agree with Kathy that our regard sinks in because it is woven into the program. Residents feel it in the small amenities of the guesthouse and studio barn. They find it in the special meals that the cooks create, in Ted's patience with a first-time rider, and in Nancy's smile at eleven-thirty on a Saturday night when she meets a resident at the airport who missed his earlier scheduled flight. Albert and I may speak our words of regard, but they are echoed in every staff member's action, every step of the way.

Most residents begin their time at Windcall adjusting to a dramatic and sometimes disorienting change of physical setting. But as the days pass, they discover that they have entered a small community where they are safe and valued. This is important because many also begin to feel the consequences of a drastic disruption in their habits and routines. They not only have been cut loose from a familiar sense of place, but also from the all-encompassing structure of their work. Suddenly they have time, emptiness, and disquieting choice.

More than a few will use the comfort and support they find here to take risks, confront hard questions, try new things, and forge different perspectives. Almost all will spend their time exploring some unfamiliar and often unexpected terrain, either physical, emotional, or both.

It's the details that create a safety zone in which we can unwind, open up, and let the restorative powers do their work:

> *—the flannel sheets and down comforters*
>
> *—the good books*
>
> *—the writings and art of former residents on the walls*
>
> *—pieces of nature on the shelf in your writing room: a stone, a bird's nest, a clump of moss*
>
> *—small delights all around.*

It's the details that create an intimacy; that make a space where we can break away from old constraints and soar.

—Donna Parson (2002)

5 What Comes Up

Being a type A personality, I work hard and I work long hours.
I am looking forward to not living under perpetual deadlines,
to-do lists, and stress. But frankly, I am a little nervous about
the prospect of having a whole month or even two weeks to
"move as the spirit moves me." I'm wondering just what will
come up if I let it.

—*Pamela Twiss,*
Windcall application (2002)

One of our earliest and most basic expectations for Windcall was that all our residents would have a restful and rejuvenating experience. Albert and I assumed that they would revel in doing nothing but their heart's desire and that when they left, they would carry with them new friendships, fresh ideas, and increased energy for their work.

Our projection wasn't entirely far-fetched. About a quarter of our residents have closely followed that scenario, quickly settling in to enjoy their unencumbered days. Our very first group, however, showed us a much more accurate picture of what would happen to the majority of our guests over the years.

Like us, this foursome expected that they would relax and reassess their efforts for social justice. But not one of them behaved quite as we — or they — had imagined. The first arrived emotionally scarred and physically spent from his decades of toil for civil rights in rural North Carolina. He covered page after page of paper with an anguished wail of poetry and prose. The second resident packed boxes of office papers but as an afterthought threw a guitar onto the backseat of his car. He had hung onto it since his teenage years, when he had toured rural Colorado in a country gospel duo. While the documents sat abandoned, he sat on the porch and strummed out some new organizing songs. The third showed up reeling from a divorce that she had been too busy to see coming. She spent her days restlessly roaming mountain trails, trying to make sense of it all. And the last of this first foursome was so ecstatic to be out from behind a desk that he spent nearly all his daylight hours outdoors with Ted and Albert, pounding nails into new fence posts and building an entry gate to the ranch. Most evenings he cleaned up and went into town to play pool.

It was suddenly clear to us that the residents' uses of Windcall would be as diverse as they were, and that most of our guests would be no better at predicting how they would spend their time than we had been. None of us could anticipate which personal needs would rise up and clamor for attention. But during that year and those that followed, we realized that most of our residents would arrive with an agenda, often unbeknownst to themselves, that would shape their days. Over time, we began to notice a few repeated themes.

The most common one resulted from our choice to make Windcall a program with no program so that residents could have significant time to themselves. Within the safe and comfortable environment we had created, we eliminated as much pressure, expectation, and obligation as we could. Except for having to show up at six in the evening for dinner, the residents were on their own.

To our initial surprise, this absence of a schedule created its own stress. These organizers and activists were going cold turkey from a life where deadlines and responsibilities structured their time hour by hour. Few if any moments remained to wander, explore, play, or learn something totally unrelated to work — in short, to do anything just for pleasure. For some, the expanse of free time they found at Windcall seemed endless and somewhat daunting. They couldn't figure out what they were supposed to do here. On her first day, one resident wrote that time passed so slowly she imagined that if she stayed at Windcall, she would never age.

Some residents quickly fill the uncomfortable void with yet another demanding structure. At sixty-three Jim Sessions seemed an easy-going and comfortable man. When he came to the program he had just left his position as the director of the Highlander Center, a Tennessee training facility known as the cradle of the civil rights movement. As it turned out, Jim was not as laid-back as he seemed. He admitted as much as he painted a picture that may be familiar to many of us.

> Too much of my life was lists; interior lists that come and go and reform in my mind; and exterior lists on paper that I took pride in checking off. It was a joyless, "stepmaster" kind of daily motion, not movement.
>
> So I came to Windcall wanting to become "listless." But dishearteningly, as soon as I arrived I started my Windcall list: to do yoga, to do horses, to hike x miles every day, to go to Yellowstone, to swim in the Boiling River, to read or write x number of pages. . . . When I tried to go without a plan, I felt disoriented, dislocated, and in disarray.

Janet Robideau also discovered how difficult it was to pull the plug on her work. An imposing American Indian woman both in height and personality, Janet organizes low-income, off-reservation Native Americans on issues of discrimination in education, employment, and law enforcement.

> I would listen to the deafening silence. That silence was so loud that it thundered and echoed in my ears. I'd be OK for a minute, an hour, and then suddenly my mind would fill with thoughts of work, work, work.

Jim and Janet's words describe what happens to many residents during their shift to sudden inactivity. They lose their bearings, get anxious, and feel the pressure to return to their base camp of constant busyness. As exhausted as they may be, they experience the absence of work as a physical deprivation. They find themselves possessed by an uncomfortable sense of emptiness and undirected nervous energy.

One day Tom di Maria was consumed by his responsibilities running the International Gay and Lesbian Human Rights Commission, and the next he was sitting in the stillness of Windcall with no agenda. He expected to feel relief but instead he experienced a different kind of distress.

In the beginning this place seems only to take from me. Absorbing my points of reference, it leaves me alone with the task of constructing my own new guideposts.

Despite being competent leaders, many residents are not used to making choices based on what they want and enjoy. In order to cope with the mountain of work that structures their days, they have ignored signals about their own needs, thereby derailing the process of feedback that informs personal choice. Faced with free time at Windcall, residents are at a loss. When they turn inward to ask for direction, they hear no answering voice.

This is one of the hidden costs of overwork. Many residents have forgotten what brings them relaxation and pleasure. As a result, they cannot recognize and reach for things that might provide some respite from their rigorous schedules. As I noticed their confusion, I began to think more deeply about the most basic mechanics of emotional self-care and the process of daily renewal.

I considered the kinds of things Albert and I consistently use to restore ourselves. We each have a variety of small, very individual, comforting rituals and activities. They become particularly important when some personal struggle or demanding commitment drains our energies. These simple things rarely fail to soothe us and raise our spirits.

Most mornings at first light I take a walk with Jesse because I know that I need the exercise, but I get more than that. I see the still undisturbed tracks of night critters in the dust or snow. I hear the sandhill cranes conversing across the valley, feel the temperature drop as the road dips down to Ross Creek, and watch one of a thousand different versions of sunrise. I usually come home smiling — all my senses humming. Once inside I take pleasure in the slow ritual of making our breakfast tea in a bright red pot. If I need to arrange a serious "time out" from some problem or another, I spend a couple of hours with my camera or my paintbrush. Either can transport me temporarily into a completely worry-free zone.

Albert has a different array of things he turns to. He listens to jazz, reaches for tools at his workbench, goes into the woods to clear trails, or takes a long bike ride. Such activities are guaranteed to settle his mind. There are days, of course, when both of us trim all such pleasures back to make room for other commitments. But we remember their value and return to them. Realizing this, I gained a new respect for the healing power of ordinary pursuits.

In their ongoing attempt to find more time to meet their myriad responsibilities, our residents routinely relinquish their own versions of these small supports. They no longer recognize the value of what they have discarded or realize that their actions have seriously undercut their ability to be self-nurturing. About two years into the program we began to see that we might help them replace those losses.

We looked anew at the residents' discomfort with the expanse of free time at Windcall and recognized an opportunity: we could take advantage of their strong motivation to do something. If their anxiety compelled them to seek out activities, we could make sure they found a variety of options in their path that would encourage them to explore and experiment. Given time, their drive to simply keep busy might be overtaken by their delight in what they discovered. Residents could begin to regroove their knowledge of what they had lost or never taken the time to try. Eventually they would identify their own small list of reliable pleasures and supports.

We soon found out that trusting and using our own experience brought good results. Any number of residents exclaimed during their residency that they had stretched their capacity for fun by riding a bike, swimming in the pond, or reading a novel — only a few of the joys that had been squeezed out of their days. They rediscovered simple things they had forgotten but used to love to do. One found the piano in the TV room of the Big Barn and remembered the central importance of music in her life. She returned with delight to a daily practice that had been set aside years before. Every afternoon for two weeks, we saddled our horses to the amazing sound of classical music.

Another year a resident recalled how much she once loved to dance and how long she had gone without that pleasure. From that point on, she spent an hour each evening alone in the soaring main space of the Big Barn — CD player at high volume, twirling and rocking to the beat. Yet another marveled when she suddenly realized she had completely forgotten that tomato juice was a favorite drink!

Regina Botterill found a brand new passion at Windcall. In Chicago she spends her working days rebuilding alliances between religious and labor communities so they can work together to improve conditions for low-wage workers. At the suggestion of a housemate at Windcall, she went on her first mountain hike. This young woman, who on the evening of her arrival had run from the silhouettes of mountains against a dark gray sky, soon became so infatuated with hiking that she set out on a different and more difficult trail each day. Before she left Windcall, she called a friend back home and made plans for a week-long hiking trip the following fall. As she wrote in her *Impressions*, she had found "a whole new part of me that I will cherish."

Along with remembered or recently discovered interests, residents also begin to reincorporate undervalued parts of themselves. They find that focusing their lives so narrowly on work has crowded out what they regarded as extraneous strengths, aptitudes, and other ways of being. Regina took home a fresh experience of her courage and physical endurance. Others reawaken a sleeping artistic creativity or simply reconnect with a solid sense of self that does not solely depend on the validation of hard work.

Many residents brave the vacuum of time and let go of their pervasive identification with work. When they do, most are rewarded with the freedom to explore, experiment, and rediscover what nourishes them. In the process they begin to forge a stronger connection to their own inner system of guidance. But others must first face what has been safely repressed by the weight of their hard and constant work schedule and now, freed abruptly, demands their attention.

I came to Windcall needing something desperately. The past several months felt like I was just spinning my wheels and the direction that I was spinning was downward. It didn't seem to matter how hard or long I worked, how much time I gave up with my family and friends: nothing could keep me from this downward spinning motion. My only solace was a little voice inside that said, "These are the worst of times." And somehow that helped.

At Windcall, I found the beginning of what I was looking for, something that would give me the strength and the courage to carry on. And most surprising to me, I found it where I never thought to look before, inside myself! That little quiet voice that spoke to me before was still there but now offering other insights, other ways of looking at things. And, the one insight that is/was most important to me is . . . slowing down. . . . The importance of being still. This is new to me. This is a beginning for me.

—Conny Ford (2005)

6 Sounds in the Silence

POND JAZZ

The buzzzzz, bass, tenor, and alto. Horse fly, dragonfly,
   darting insects.
Each bird takes a phrase, a melody, repeats, answers.
The occasional splat, splash, slap
(a guest appearance from the fish).
Horse snorts a bass line.
This song is so compelling, I put the book down and listen.

—*Bob Hudek (2001)*

*t*he mountains surrounding our small ranch rise to 9,600 feet, and the valley to the west is nearly the size of Rhode Island. When residents first arrive, the silence at Windcall can seem just as vast. As they relax and their ears adjust, however, they begin to tune into a natural din: the music of birds, insects, animals, the wind. Most residents are amazed and delighted by the concert.

But some are bombarded instead by a cacophony. They hear only urgent inner voices assailing them with needs that they didn't expect. These individuals have held grief and mourning at bay by working nonstop. When they slow their pace at Windcall, their submerged feelings rise and threaten to engulf them. Like our early resident who was facing a surprise divorce, they, too, must make peace with an important personal loss. They mourn a neglected relationship that has slipped away, a parent or friend who has died. A few grieve for a child or young adult killed in the streets.

During her residency, Kay Whitlock performed a private, starlight ceremony to honor almost forty friends and coworkers who had died of AIDS.

> I have felt as if I've been watching an old-growth forest come down,
> tree by tree, and have been helpless to stop it. Now it was time, finally,
> to mourn for all those who had been lost and to remember them fully.
> The tears came, and the love.

Over the last thirty years, Jaribu Hill has been a political activist and singer, and a human rights organizer. She has also raised two daughters. One of them died of an aneurysm in 1997. During her recent residency Jaribu wrote:

> For seven years I have known the loss and grief of losing a child. The
> organizing work was there to propel me back into life. I worked, I
> drove myself, and I kept on hiding. When I first got to Windcall, the
> edge around me was thick and the fear of self-discovery was paralyzing.
> I did not want to think about me. I wanted to keep running. And then
> I found the strength inside.

No one who dares to care for someone else is safe from personal loss. Hard work is a common and very effective anesthetic for the resulting pain. When you toil until exhaustion, little room is left for feelings and memories. But at Windcall, it is particularly hard for residents to continue to avoid their sorrow. There is too much natural beauty that tugs at their emotions, too many moments that demand their vulnerability. And there is too much empty time. The natural process of healing has a chance to take hold, pushing them back into the pain, guiding them down the only path that will temper and eventually transform their trauma.

Some residents must face a different kind of distress, one that results not from personal loss but from frequent contact with the misery and oppression of others. Their work exposes them to deeply troubling inhumanities. They organize in sweatshops where immigrant women work nine-hour days to earn less than half the federal poverty level, or in fields where the children of farm-workers play in pesticide-contaminated water. They watch as third-generation family farmers lose homes and land to foreclosure, or they witness the disastrous human and environmental effects of unregulated industrial dumping. In time, these workers for social justice pay a price. They absorb and carry an ongoing sadness.

Diane Bady is one of the leaders of a coalition of groups in West Virginia that works to restrict a highly destructive coal-mining technique that removes the entire tops of mountains. This practice has annihilated hundreds of thousands of acres of mountains, streams, and valuable hardwood forests. The mud and water from flooding also have damaged the homes of coalfield residents. Diane explains the cost of this degradation to those working to stop it.

> Many activist leaders deal with grief every day. We see human and ecological injustice. And it hurts. Ideally, this pain is transformed into the energy that fuels our work. But often, the intensity of our lives keeps too much of the pain buried deep in our hearts and in our over-stressed bodies.

Christina Jose-Kampfner bears a residue of sorrow from her work with incarcerated mothers and their children. The week before she came to Windcall, she accompanied a fourteen-year-old boy on his Saturday visit. This time he refused to hug his mother good-bye and Christina asked him why. He answered that he was afraid that if he put his arms around her, he would be unable to let her go. Christina wrote:

> My heart sunk in the face of so much pain. Living among these feelings makes it very difficult to feel my own. At Windcall I have looked inside myself and dealt with feelings I did not know I had. I have kept a river of tears inside me.

For residents like these, it takes incredible energy to ignore or navigate around this stored emotion. Once they are able to set it free and their grief abates, they experience a new surge of vitality. The internal structure they have built to contain their pain has imprisoned much more than intended.

In a similar way, a few residents find themselves confronting a specific fear that they have avoided. One resident who organized in the housing projects in Chicago was terrified by the darkness at Windcall, where only a flashlight or the moon can brighten the path at night. Back in her neighborhood, where street violence was always a threat, darkness indeed held danger. But even though she knew that there was little peril at Windcall, she was afraid to go out alone after the sun set. Her specific and appropriate fear had become generalized and was untouched by reason or a change of circumstance.

She set a goal of walking alone at night from the big barn to the guest-house and she worked toward it with determination. The day after she succeeded, she was elated. She had experienced the joy of walking home slowly in safety with nothing to illuminate her way but a canopy of stars and no sound other than her own footsteps on the gravel path. More importantly, she became aware of the weight of anxiety she carried from living in a dangerous place and realized that she needed to take that burden seriously and find ways, from time to time, to get away and put it down.

Another resident was horrified on arrival to see Jesse, who, with tail-wagging pleasure, bounded to meet her. She fled back into the safety of her car. An accomplished world traveler who lectured and consulted on college and high school integration issues, she had been terrified of dogs since childhood. On her second day at Windcall, she told me she would have to leave. I struck a deal with her: I would incarcerate Jesse for certain hours of the day so that she would be able to walk outside without fear of running into him. Though skeptical that I would remember to hold to our bargain, she agreed to try.

For the first few days she could only venture a short distance before hastily returning to the guesthouse in panic. But gradually her accumulated successes began to erode the old but powerful certainty of disaster that had controlled her for so many years.

On one of her last days, our guest's newly found freedom was unexpectedly tested. A friend came to visit me and let his dog out of the car at our gate so the animal could run the rest of the way to our house to get some exercise. Our resident was sitting and reading in the sun on the studio barn porch when she saw the strange dog galloping up the driveway. It took a moment for her to realize that she felt none of her familiar terror.

Although this resident did not apply to Windcall with any notion of confronting her phobia of dogs, that powerful fear, once aroused, demanded to be addressed. She, like many of her compatriots, had little choice but to listen.

In the quiet of their Windcall days, many residents discover less urgent but still persistent anxieties — often about the future. They face choices and transitions for which they may feel ill-prepared. Residents of both sexes have struggled with their hope to balance their desire to have a family with their continued commitment to social justice. The two do not easily go together. Each can demand full attention and the combination has left more than one organizer feeling inadequate at both.

Several women have spent a good deal of time at Windcall thinking about their approaching menopause and its larger meaning. They ponder how their relationship to their work should reflect their aging process. Some consider leaving direct organizing and focusing instead on mentoring others. That change would honor both their diminishing energy and their accumulated wisdom. But they are used to the immediacy and excitement of front-line work. They are accustomed to a tangible confirmation of their value and they wonder if they can and want to give up such rewards.

In a similar way, activists or organizers who have founded and shepherded an organization for many years wrestle with how to turn it over to younger leadership. Releasing control over an entity that they have birthed and nourished for decades can be a wrenching process. It is hard to let go of their long investment of energy and heart, knowing that their creation will evolve in new directions and be guided by different priorities than their own.

In Windcall's silence, residents can listen to their feelings about such difficult, impending transitions. The wide-open vistas seem to encourage them to take the long view of their personal journey, to ask questions like: "Is this the direction I still choose?" "What is missing that I need?" "Is it time for me to move on?"

Sometimes residents find that the urgent question that fills the silence concerns their feelings about themselves. Since 1985 Jennifer Grant has worked both locally and nationally on domestic violence. At Windcall she discovered that her emphasis on her job had resulted in a neglected and uneasy relationship with herself. In fact, her greatest fear about coming had been that she would find her own company hard to endure.

> I think I've been so used to filling every second of my time — both to avoid my thoughts and feelings, and to not be wasting valuable time — that being with me seemed like something alien, something distasteful, something difficult.

Jennifer was far from the only resident who initially worried about who she would discover when she began to slow down. Over time, being too busy can become an unconscious excuse to sidestep uncomfortable feelings and challenging personal problems. Furthermore, it seems easier and certainly feels much better to help others than to take a hard look at our own rough edges. The trouble is that the longer we use that escape hatch, the more certain we become that we ourselves are worth escaping.

Another Jennifer, Jennifer Gordon, organized Latino immigrants to fight for just working conditions in low-wage industries on Long Island. She also was worried about being alone but later wrote about the surprising relief she found as she released the emotional weight of her work.

> The best thing for me, the thing that got into my very bones and the knots in my brain and eased them the way yoga eased my muscles, was to have no one need me. No one. Not the people I work with, not the immigrants who make up our center, not my lover, not my family. What a gift. It was like I learned how to breathe again.

Other residents are amazed by the difference between who they are at work and the person they see emerging at Windcall. They find new meaning in the phrase "losing yourself in your work" as they rediscover playful parts of themselves that have been long buried by responsibility.

Cindy Marano spent her working days trying to improve and expand job opportunities for low-income women in Oakland, California. She met a different version of herself at Windcall, one that she had not let loose for a long time. She set aside the earnest and concerned forty-nine-year-old, the issue expert, the serious analyzer, the judge and worrier.

I was a child for two weeks. I allowed myself sheer wonder. I swam joyously in the pond. I ran singing down hills and put my bare feet into cold, bubbling streams. I picked wildflowers. I experimented with allowing myself to witness life anew.

Many of Cindy's fellow residents find a similar playfulness that delights them. They discover a light and humorous side they had forgotten but gratefully welcome back. Most begin to realize how their work has made them define too narrowly what parts of themselves have importance and value. They confront their own secret concern about how, over their years of incessant work, they have become strangers to themselves.

Eventually all residents are able to listen with pleasure to the layers of sound that make up the silence at Windcall. They also may hear from an expanded, more interesting and diverse self and, in fact, be hard-pressed to keep up with the explosion of creativity and expressiveness that often follows.

There are plenty of things at this place that just envelop you into prolonged submission: the radiant sunsets, the fluorescent moon coming up behind the mountains, the rustling of the woods, the silky water of the pond! And the beds (oh, the beds!) are soft and always inviting. And definitely, you should submit with wild abandon. It is time to feel the turbulence inside of each of us—what makes us do the things that we do, those things that facilitate or retard our own growth. Windcall has gone very deep into my soul and allowed me to hear the turbulence and the tranquility like I've never heard it before.

—Francis Calpotura (1996)

7 The Studio Barn

*My senses begin to open up and take in more. After an
evening rain shower, my nostrils dilate with the rich smell
of earth and water and manure. I notice more gradations
of color in the hills, more tones of green on the trees. This
land overwhelms me and crowds out other thoughts.*

—*Beverly Bell (2003)*

*t*he studio barn sits on a grassy rise just beyond a thicket of hawthorn and
aspen below the guesthouse. Inside, on the walls of its two art studios, residents have thumbtacked a riot of pencil drawings, watercolors, acrylic paintings, and papier-mâché masks. Brightly painted rocks, stick creatures, and
clay bowls of various shapes and degrees of symmetry sit on a table near the
potter's wheel. Along the walls of the hallway, artwork gives way to a display
of poems and prose near the doors of four individual studies. Each room has
a comfortable reading chair and a desk with a computer and drawers full of
paper and sharpened pencils.

The idea to provide our residents with art studios and private writing
rooms came directly from my own early years on the property. Every time I
returned, the stillness and beauty of the land deeply affected me: all my senses
were heightened and I was propelled into a flurry of creativity.

First I tried to catch on film every view and change of light on the
mountains and fields. When the late afternoon sun gilded the landscape, I
shoved cooking pots to the back of the stove and ran to capture it. When dawn

turned new snow pink on the tops of the Bridger Mountains, I was out in my slippers before it paled. Later I produced poem after poem about this incredible place — wanting to express the intense feelings it evoked, to record my reconnection to the land and the heady sense of aliveness that filled me.

Remembering those days, I felt certain that many residents would have a similar experience. Leaving behind work that was intense and unrelenting, they, too, could be moved by this magnificent landscape. In the sudden quiet, they might discover and want to give voice to new ideas and feelings.

Two years into the project, we built the studio barn to encourage and nourish this process. Within its rooms, organizers and activists revisit something they may have abandoned to the demands of their jobs: creative expression. Sometimes the potter's wheel turns all day and into the evening; words spill out on the page; paints flow across the canvas or onto found objects. For many residents, the studio barn best catches whatever has been freed by the absence of work.

While I was assembling the supplies for the art rooms, I found myself thinking about the central role of play in child development. It is the first way we explore our environment and its possibilities. Those thoughts led me to expand my idea of the materials I wanted to provide for the residents. In addition to traditional adult media, I added finger paints, fat marking pencils, colorful textured and printed papers, scissors, and paste — the kinds of things that enthrall my grandkids. Knowing the goal-oriented, pressured days that fill our residents' lives, I wanted some stuff that would be hard to take seriously — things that would invite "fooling around."

It worked. Using these tools and objects from nature, residents begin to explore and play. Some pick up pieces of gnarled twigs and roots and create fantastic, painted creatures with many legs and eyes. Others decorate rocks or walking sticks, and one used the skull of a long-deceased cow as his canvas. These artists laugh a lot and marvel at their childlike creations.

Residents also try to capture the physical beauty of their environment with crayons, paints, and pastels. In a variety of representational and abstract forms, they record their responses to the land. Alexa Bradley codirected a coalition in Minnesota that brought together many progressive constituencies, including union members, environmentalists, people of color, women, and seniors, to find common ground for joint community action. In the studio barn, she picked up some paints and got lost in a new adventure.

> Yesterday I discovered watercolors, the lush flow of color in water, and I can't stop myself.
> Sky sky sky on paper.

Creating in the studio barn offers a rare freedom to these organizers and activists usually so concerned with efficiency and measurable results: they can lose themselves in the process of spreading rich color or kneading the slick coolness of the clay. A good belly laugh might be the measure of success. Residents can do something for the sheer pleasure of it and for the healthy escape from weightier matters that such activities provide.

Long ago a resident tacked two of her delicate and detailed drawings of native grasses to the wall of one art room. When I look at them, I imagine the act of seeing that had to precede each sketch, the attention required before the artist's hand could even begin to move. And long after she left the studio barn, she probably continued to notice exquisite lines and shapes in abundance. It would be impossible to see a single stalk of wheat grass so accurately without also feeling a heightened awareness of everything else she encountered.

Back home in Durham, North Carolina, Betsy Barton focused on fighting for improved workplace safety for low-income wage earners. One afternoon at Windcall she sat in a pasture completely absorbed in the task of sketching several wild irises. As she was noticing the subtleties of color and shape, the bud she was observing popped open, unfolding petal by petal in front of her eyes. Betsy marveled at being slowed down and still enough to witness and celebrate that small miracle.

Other residents find art and writing to be effective tools for releasing old, jammed-up feelings. Gloria Simoneaux runs a program for homeless children. She uses art to help them express the hardships of their disrupted family life. When she tried to deal with her own work-related grief, she found that a tactile and nonverbal expression worked best for her, too. Gloria painted a series of self-portraits during her stay. The first one was in shadowed shades of blues and grays that clearly revealed the exhaustion and mourning that filled her. Gradually the portraits became more colorful and whimsical. Her final portrait is painted in all colors of the spectrum.

Excited by the prospect of forming something with their own hands, some residents are particularly drawn to the potter's wheel. Michelle Orton, a young mother of two sons, is a neighbor — and a potter herself — who has come to Windcall to give lessons. She, her husband, and two young sons spend most weekends hiking, camping, or mountain biking. Michelle is a gifted teacher — equally creative with our seven-year-old granddaughter and the most seasoned organizers. Even with her help, though, residents sometimes find the process of throwing a pot intimidating. Most only relax when they see our collection of other beginners' works. These pieces express clearly that perfection is not the point.

For anyone, forming a pot on the wheel can be a task of many dimensions. First, a potter must prepare the clay by slamming it hard on a board, folding it over, and slamming it again. At the start, residents are tentative; they need encouragement. But after two or three throws, all timidity evaporates and they continue with gusto.

Once the clay is positioned on the wheel, it takes strength, sustained focus, and steady hands to center it firmly in place so that the centrifugal force of the wheel can work to form the pot. If residents maintain their concentration, they can feel and see the bowl emerge magically between their hands. But if they let the clay get out of balance, it begins to wobble madly and may even go flying across the room. More than one person, tongue in cheek, has drawn the parallel between the fate of the off-center clay and what happens when their own lives get seriously out of balance.

During his month-long stay, Ruben Nunez spent many hours at the potter's wheel. When he went back home to New Mexico, where he organizes in the desperately poor *colonias* on the Mexican border, he took with him more than pieces of pottery.

> I learned something related to organizing. You need patience to see results, and as soon as you want to make things in a hurry, you will see your mistake. And even after you finish your bowl or cup, you need to make the final touches in order to appreciate your efforts. Clay is the

community of people and you work to give it form, but you don't know what is going to result until all the work is complete. You provide a process for them to become something beautiful.

Attorney Diane Chin had reached a point in her work with hate crimes and police misconduct where she had begun to question her own efficacy, resilience, and abilities. When she came to Windcall, she was physically and emotionally exhausted and wondering if she could continue. She found relief and new energy in the studio barn and advised future residents to try the same prescription.

MAKE ART! Play with this stuff! Take out your frustrations wedging and pounding clay. Encourage your child-self and squeeze paints on something and finger paint. Make at least one thing that you want to take with you that will bring you back to this place and at least one thing that you want to leave here to encourage others to play.

Just a few steps from the two art studios, a hall leads to four small writing rooms. There is one for each resident to use during his or her stay. In our early years of running the program, we referred to these spaces as "offices." Then, a few years ago over dinner in the guesthouse, we were asked an interesting question. Someone inquired why we provided offices when it was obvious in other ways that we hoped residents wouldn't spend time here working. We realized that our language had not kept pace with the program's evolution. We had long since happily noticed that the "offices" were seldom used primarily for work, despite the original expectations of many of their occupants.

Elizabeth Ainsley Campbell arrived obviously determined to make productive use of her time. Three large boxes of files from her Boston-based environmental nonprofit and her national peace and justice organization had preceded her. We were dismayed to see that she had brought so much work along, but we needn't have worried. Elizabeth managed to unpack only half of one box before becoming completely distracted. It was June and every field and hillside was extravagant with wildflowers. Elizabeth was seized by an unexpected passion to find, identify, and record as many as she could. She left

Windcall a month later relaxed and satisfied, carrying her carefully completed book of annotated and exquisitely rendered wildflower watercolors. UPS handled the boxes.

Although some residents do spend part of their time here creating organizational strategies and long-range plans, most use their rooms as a private space to explore and express themselves through poetry, stories and reflections. So, spurred on by our dinner companion's question, we decided it was high time to change the offices to writing studios both in name and atmosphere.

Our daughter Melissa knows more about color and creating intriguing and welcoming environments than anyone I know, so I asked her to join me with the project. We went off together to search the local second-hand shops and returned with a car full of things to help in the transformation. We found worn but still beautiful handmade quilts to hang on the walls, old tin boxes and trays in warm colors to hold pencils and paper clips, glass bottles, a few woven baskets, and pillows and throws for the reading chairs. We found small wooden packing crates to use as side tables and loaded them up with paperbacks about identifying birds, star constellations, animal tracks and scat. We put our three favorite books about creative writing on the hall table and added a dictionary and thesaurus to each room. We hung shelves for found objects and bulletin boards for snapshots. Although the rooms still had a desk and computer, they now issued a very different invitation.

Residents seemed to enjoy the creative push. David Mann found his writing room to be the most important place at Windcall. In San Carlos, California, he led a multi-denominational group of congregations working together to improve conditions in their low-income neighborhoods. Here he spent hours at his desk recording a stream of poetry that bubbled up like an underground spring. He said that a poet inside had been patiently waiting for the chance to emerge.

Cate Poe had spent seventeen years as a labor and community organizer. For more than a decade of that time she organized and trained low- and moderate-income parents who wanted to make a difference in their children's schools. In her own writing room, she could barely keep up with all that she wanted to express:

At Windcall, I wrote stories almost every day. I don't know how this magic worked. I just know it was such fun to plop down at the computer, take a deep breath, and have the words tumble out, like a bunch of kids bursting loose at the end of a school year.

There have even been a few residents who, like me, felt all their senses reawaken and clamor for expression. When he arrived, Steve Lew was working with HIV-positive Asian and Pacific Islanders in a community-based program in San Francisco. He wrote a poem describing how each of his senses responded to Windcall. Here are three segments:

What I smelled:
My sweat in cold air
Wet dog
Wood fire smoke.

What I touched:
Place mats and cloth napkins
Soft horse mane
Brushes   paint   canvas   writing journal.

What I heard:
Lots of voices in restoration
The sound of my heart questioning my voice
The wind hurling snowballs against the house.

Writing often leads to deeper thoughts, and so it did for some residents. They begin by recording experiences and feelings and end up asking hard questions about their lives. Many search for ways to do meaningful work in the world, be responsive to the plight of others, and yet not lose themselves. By reconnecting to their own creativity, they gain a deeper sense of who that self is.

It took writing this book to make me understand the explosion of my own senses and creativity that had occurred at Windcall. Now I realize that I was actually the first resident. When I arrived, I drastically altered the usual composition of my life. I exchanged the structured hours of my private practice and teaching for long periods with no schedule at all. I left my office and spent time in nature. I traded a daily concentration on the needs of clients and family for attention to my own perceptions and feelings. My familiar relationships to time, place, and my own abilities were drastically shuffled and in their repositioning I regained a joyful, creative voice.

This discovery is the real gift of the studio barn. By exploring the invitations there, residents are able to reincorporate the part of themselves that remembers how to play, gets happily lost in making something, and delights in the senses. They learn that taking time to notice, develop, and record their own vision is more than a luxury. Self-expression is a healing force.

Many leave Windcall vowing to continue their creative writing, pottery, or painting because those activities provide a refuge, feed a fresh perspective, and generate energy that can revitalize all parts of their lives — even, and perhaps especially, their work.

More importantly, the opportunities for fun, emotional release, and artistic expression in the studio barn contribute to a larger goal of the Windcall program. They further strengthen the residents' relationships to themselves, relationships that have been seriously frayed by an overriding focus on the needs of others.

What I gained was a deeper faith in the creative energy latent and moving in us all—waiting, hungering for an invitation, an opening.

—Alexa Bradley (1998)

(No) Clay Words

In the beginning, there are words and meanings.
Things to remember from the teacher. Notes must be taken.
Wedge it. Throw it into squares. 100 tosses.
Center yourself. (Yeah, sure, no problem.)
Arms at 10 and 2. Right arm firm, anchored to body.
Push up, cone, palm flat, push down.
Thumbs into center. Forefingers hooked, pull straight out.
Now pull it up. Bottom dry. Rim held firm.
There are the tools, wires cut, bat holds, the needle measures,
The thingamajigs trim.
Under glazes, clear glazes, drying times.
So many words.

After awhile, the words disappear.
Words don't count here. It's the feeling, the awareness,
The movement . . .
Firm, wet slippery, all texture
Nervous, funny, sexy.
The sounds of slamming to wedge, squishing to center,
The whir of the machine.
A moment when it is locked in, happy, centered.
Lost in time, utterly absorbed.
Each time something new is learned.
Is there a product for the world?
Does it matter?

—Bob Hudek (2001)

8 Trails and Trials

I gave myself up to Truman Gulch—kicking through the
pine-needled dirt, brushing past the leaves that were green,
then yellow, stepping through the stream, feeling warm air
slide to cool. That was enough. That was everything.

—*Karen Lehman (1996)*

Standing on the front porch of the guesthouse, residents may choose from a variety of walking options. Straight ahead to the west, a short uphill trail leads to the large pastures where, at dawn and dusk, the local elk herd often comes to graze. Up beyond our house to the left, the gently rolling wooded acres of the ranch beckon. Every spring my industrious husband clears paths there that meander under huge old firs and through groves of aspen.

At our highest fence line, Albert has linked well-traveled animal trails with flagged switchbacks to mark a route that climbs sixteen hundred feet and follows the ridge directly above Windcall. It is about a three-and-a-half-hour hike to the summit and back, including a stop for a picnic lunch and time to admire spectacular views in all directions.

Walking downhill from the guesthouse, residents can follow a wildflower-festooned slope to the pond or take the driveway to the front gate, from where the Truman Gulch trail into the National Forest is only a few minutes' trek. Particularly for our urban guests, it is a miracle to simply walk out the door and have immediate access to nature and uninterrupted time alone.

Walking, however, turns out to be one of several unexpected and blunt teachers. At Windcall, residents have time to notice their bodies and many discover that they are in a state of neglect: out of shape and overweight. These folks climb the small hill to watch for elk and soon find that they are short of breath. Or they take a half-hour walk in the woods and their hamstrings and knee joints sharply remind them how long it has been since they have had any regular exercise.

Others receive a similar message in the Tuesday morning yoga sessions. At seven-thirty in the morning, residents can join a group of neighbors who meet for a weekly class in the big barn. A teacher from Bozeman drives out for the ninety-minute lesson; she is particularly adept at working with people of different skill levels. Since the class became an option, more and more residents have chosen to attend. While they may enjoy the challenge, some are stunned to discover how tight and inflexible they are and how elusive a sturdy sense of balance can be.

Many of our residents are in the habit of ignoring warning signals from their bodies. They block out messages that might slow them down and demand time they don't think they have to spare. Instead they draw deeply on their internal strength and passion to keep going.

Karen Narasaki, for example, had made a plan for her time in residency: she was going to ponder the direction her Asian-American community was heading and determine how to reposition her organization so it could better meet changing needs. Instead, without the insistent demands of work to keep her distracted, she was confronted by the needs of her own body. Although she knew she was diabetic, Karen had put off improving her diet and getting more exercise. Regular medical checkups were also at the bottom of her list. Her health scarcely seemed important when compared to her community's needs. But when she tried to walk for any distance around Windcall, the discomfort and exhaustion she felt spoke loudly of her neglect.

Other residents show a similar disregard for monitoring and caring for their physical health. Clearly, the ethos of self-sacrifice still persists — that for a just cause, organizers and activists should be willing, as the old saying goes, to "die with their boots on." Many ignore the important relationship between good physical condition and sustained, effective, and creative leadership. In addition, they fail to remember the connection between individual and organizational health.

Karen changed her course three days into her residency. She began to take daily walks. Hiking at this altitude of 5,500 feet was a big challenge, but with the support of a fellow resident, she persisted. Since she couldn't go very far at first, she had to scale down her expectations substantially. But her new regime slowly produced its own reinforcement. She steadily began to feel stronger, and as a bonus she gained important insights to apply to her work life when she got home.

> The destination is not always the point! The journey is often what is more important. It is okay to stop and rest rather than to push through the pain. It is okay to take on a challenge that you are uncertain you can meet. If you go slow and do it in stages, the challenge is always manageable.

As residents begin to get reacquainted with their own long-ignored bodies, they also set goals for themselves. After all, these are people who are used to accepting challenges. Many enjoy the summons to improve their endurance and it isn't long before they realize that their efforts strengthen more than muscles.

When he began his residency, Joel Shufro had already spent eighteen years combating the occupational hazards that threaten the health and safety of workers in New York City. Joel walked into the mountains every day and pushed himself to his physical limit.

> Being alone in the backcountry might not seem frightening to you, but for someone who has spent the last twenty-seven years in the heart of New York City, it was close to traumatic. I was terrified of being caught in an electrical storm at the top of a mountain, of meeting a bear, or of falling and injuring myself. Pushing myself made me come to grips with some of my own personal fears. Each day, I felt more confident and empowered.

Like Joel did, when we try something new and succeed, we gain more than another pleasant activity to pursue. Our whole feeling about ourselves gets an extra boost.

We also benefit from having in our lives some work or activities where success is easily measured. When I was a young wife and mother, I actually looked forward to balancing my checkbook. It was the rare task that had a beginning, an end, and a right answer. With three kids under five, most of my work didn't meet those criteria. It came unraveled by day's end and needed to be done all over again, whereas in my monthly mathematical task, I could enjoy a quick, definitive triumph. Our residents' work seldom has a tidy, discernible end either. When they reach the top of a mountain or return from their first horseback ride, they feel the same fine sense of accomplishment that balancing my checkbook never failed to provide.

Physical exertion often takes residents out of their heads and away from constant strategizing and planning. Instead they can focus on the moment and the interactions between their bodies and their immediate surroundings. Many reawaken senses that have been numbed and clouded by the pace of their lives. Dianne D'Arrigo found that kind of sensory renewal by swimming in the pond, where she was able to leave behind the work on industrial environmental pollution that had claimed her efforts since the late 1970s. She advised future summer residents to jump into the pond every day.

> The pond is amniotic. Swim the perimeter to smell the wild roses and other flower scents wafting in and out with the barnyard aromas and sounds. Float in the middle to forget the world and just be. Dive deep to feel the temperature changes. Don't worry if it's rainy or cold — it is only a four-minute walk up through the wildflower path to the guest-house and a hot shower or bath, tea or killer coffee, warm clothes, and maybe the hammock and a book.

Jonathan Polansky was one of our first residents, the one who mended fences and indulged his passion for playing pool. His work usually kept him behind a desk devising ad campaigns for nonprofits. Jonathan also frequented the pond, but at a chillier time of year and long before we added the small beach. He issued a warning to those residents who were brave enough to follow his lead.

This is a spring-fed pond, which means that a foot below the surface a cold hand awaits you. Going in off the mud may remind you of childhood quicksand terrors, but leaping off the dock will send your whole life unreeling before your eyes. Your choice. But do it regardless.

Some residents feel that getting on a horse is just as reckless as jumping into an icy pond. Many have never ridden before. Of those who have, almost all seem to have been younger than age ten and had terrifying experiences. Thanks to Ted's gentle persistence and the powerful written urgings of past residents, however, almost everyone who comes to Windcall gives riding a try.

Ted has raised most of our horses and schooled all of them. While no steed is 100 percent predictable, ours are as close as they come. I know for sure because I learned to ride on many of them. I was neither wealthy nor rural enough to grow up with horses, but as a preteen that didn't stop me from reading every horse story I could find.

When I finally lived in equine country, though, I thought that being in my mid-fifties made me too old to learn to ride. I certainly felt too old to risk falling off. Ted didn't even attempt to talk me out of my misgivings. He simply kept inviting me to come with him when he rode around to check on his cows or just enjoy the land. Since there was no speed attached to those meanderings and I just had to sit and steer, I agreed.

I remember one very unusual August dawn when a cold front had come in and we woke to find four inches of snow covering everything. Ted suggested a ride, so we filled a thermos with hot coffee and headed into the forest. As the sun rose and the temperature climbed, we watched the fir trees release showers of melting snow. Later, the woods steamed and looked as magical as any childhood fantasy I had ever imagined. I was hooked.

In the beginning years of the program, we started residents right out with a trail ride. There is little risk involved when Ted leads a string of horses walking nose to tail. In those days I often rode shotgun at the end of the line. One day we took a path where a fallen aspen leaned rider-high across the way. Ted and his followers walked around it, but the last resident and I were some yards behind. Since there was room for a horse to pass below the hazard, my companion's steed headed straight for it. Suddenly I heard a series of loud and very worried uh-oh's. I yelled at the rider to turn his mount to the right but he didn't respond. As he neared the trunk, I bellowed "whoa" to his horse, which brought them both to a standstill.

It had never occurred to Ted and me that our riders might not have the slightest notion of how to steer and fail to mention it. Now we don't assume anything. Our first ride begins in the outdoor arena with Ted instructing residents on the basics: how to stop, start, turn both ways, and back up. Then, once the riders seem fairly comfortable, he leads the group up the trail.

Riding turns out to be an important part of most residents' time here. For some it is the best part — not always, however, for the same reasons. One resident with multiple sclerosis could not easily walk for any distance. We persuaded her to give riding a try and much to her astonishment, she experienced a minimum of discomfort. She was elated to be able to accompany her housemates into the forest.

Lora Jo Foo's first ride started ominously. Nothing about her difficult work educating garment workers about their rights or holding manufacturers accountable had prepared Lora Jo for sitting astride a horse.

The first time I tried mounting one of Windcall's horses, he looked huge. For five-foot-one-inch me, he was too tall to mount without a boost. Once up, I was looking down at the world from a height of eight feet! Initially, it was very disconcerting.

Little did Lora Jo know how far her riding adventures would take her.

I never managed to get full control over Trimmer. That's because my philosophical ambivalence about the right of a 105-pound human being to assert authority over a 1,200-pound horse never resolved itself in the four weeks I was here. Still, riding Trimmer up to 7,650-foot

Ross Peak pass and eight hours later, bathing, brushing, and grooming him, was the highlight of my stay. This city girl fell in love with a horse.

Some formidable leaders in the social justice field have to muster a great deal of courage to get on a horse. Riding a large live animal is unlike anything else. Most beginners immediately stiffen at the unusual motion of a four-legged walking gait. I often suggest that they watch the haunches of the horse in front of them so they can get used to the rock-and-roll rhythm of his movements. But mainly I offer distracting conversation to help them relax a little so their bodies can learn by the feel of it. Beginners have to come to the realization that, surprisingly, riding is in large part a cooperative venture rather than entirely one of mastery.

After watching so many organizers and activists ride for the first time, I can't help thinking that despite any initial difficulties they encounter, taking on a challenge just for fun must be exhilarating. Too often, so many others depend on the results of their efforts. At Windcall they can take a risk unencumbered by the worry that their success or failure will be crucial to someone else. They can honor their fears, experiment, and then proceed only as far as they want. Nobody cares when they decide to head back to the barn.

Once again Albert and I saw that the most significant trail for residents at Windcall was the one that led them to themselves. Hiking, yoga, swimming in the pond, and horseback riding reacquainted them with their physical beings. They recognized bodies that needed use and care, senses that were deadened by overwork, and attention so tied up in responsibility for the future that it often missed the joy of the present. They also rediscovered another source of renewal in the warm success of developing or improving physical skills: by hiking to the end of the trail, holding a difficult yoga pose, or moving in synchronicity with a horse, many found a vitality and pleasure that had long been missing in their daily lives.

More than one resident has compared Windcall to a summer camp for activists and organizers. They find similarities in the kinds of physical activities we offer and the fact that they have fellow campers. It has been a long time, if ever, since most of them have done such things as spend an entire afternoon exploring the woods or practicing communication skills with a horse. But the summer camp image also reflects something else. In the unusual freedom of Windcall, many reclaim an energy, openness, and sense of possibility that they associate with a younger, more idealistic self — the same self that first took on the work of social change. Residents may also redis-cover some unexpected rewards that can come from sharing an adventure with good company.

Windcall gave me the opportunity to climb the ridge behind the house and reach the top and be rewarded by a clearing filled with wildflowers and a view of the Gallatin Valley. To hike up Truman Gulch and cross streams created by melting snow and breathe fresh air that cleared my lungs and mind. To get on a horse and go farther than I could have on foot and see things from a different perspective. To feel yoga push my body in ways that I had not thought possible and begin to sense a new relationship between my body and my mind.

—Triana Silton (2000)

I have come to
Connect
To ground
To root myself
To that which is
Unchanging
Immovable
Essential.

And so I watch Ross Peak
That mountain
To better understand
How to stand
When the sun moves and
The light changes
When the clouds close or
Part
When the rain carries hail
And threatens
When the wind is angry
How to stand
Rooted to the eternal
Grounded in the essential.

—Stewart Acuff (1999)

9 The Dinner Table

*The four of us residents were an incongruous posse on
horseback and a plucky, if winded, Outward Bound platoon
of hikers led by mountain man Albie Wells. We were city
slickers at the rodeo, politicos discussing strategy over drinks
and country western two-stepping tunes at Little John's in
Bozeman. And most of all we were new friends sharing our
stories at the dinner table.*

—Ellen Moore (1995)

*a*t around five o'clock each afternoon, residents wander in from the studio barn or arrive home from hikes to congregate in the living room. They chat with the cook or catch up with one another as enticing smells from the kitchen intensify, arousing their appetites and their speculations about what's for dinner. The six o'clock evening gathering is the only scheduled event on their daily calendar.

Jean Idell Smalls is a mother and grandmother who has directed an organization dedicated to strengthening the self-image of teenage girls in the South Carolina Sea Islands. Many are ashamed of speaking the Gullah dialect, a nonstandard form of English used by descendants of slaves. Idell helped them to write a play in the Gullah language about the lives of their grandparents. They took *In Celebration of Us* on the road and performed it in four southern states, ending up in Washington, D.C.

Dinner at Windcall, for Idell, was a reoccurring miracle. There was not a mountain or vista that matched the magnificence of having someone else prepare her supper night after night. Sometimes she would pull her chair into the kitchen so as not to miss a single moment of the work she did not have to do. Over the years we found that many women who must combine family responsibilities with their efforts for social justice share Idell's feelings. They are overjoyed to be relieved of the ongoing job of meal planning and food buying and preparation.

For all residents, in fact, mealtime ranks near the top of any list of memorable Windcall events. They rave about the food. Their uniform enthusiasm is high praise for the cooks who face new challenges with each group. Kay and her colleagues accommodate both vegetarians and meat-and-potato lovers, but sometimes they also must avoid all dairy products, wheat, nuts, or any number of other allergenic foods. Kay has been known to spend hours in the Bozeman library researching special recipes that can't be found in her own extensive collection.

Residents explain that it is not just the taste of the food that amazes them. It is the extra care and effort conveyed through the variety, creativity, and visual presentation of each meal. Pamela Twiss was the resident who was "a little nervous" about what she might find in the emptiness of her time at Windcall. In addition to being a wife and the mother of an energetic five-year-old boy, she directs a Minnesota-based organization of churches working for economic and racial justice. Pamela praised Kay's talents with these words:

> If I could cook like Kay, no one in my family would ever want to go to
> a restaurant again. Or wonder if they were loved.

Satisfied residents fill the *Impressions* books with votes for favorite meals. Some take photographs of the dinner table laden with such favorites as seafood pasta, plates of grilled garden vegetables, steaming bowls of soup swirled with herbs, and desserts like fresh peach pie or flourless chocolate cake drizzled with homemade caramel sauce. Kay brings many of the vegetables and herbs from her own garden. Recipes are available for those who ask, but the most frequent request we hear from residents is that Kay assemble a complete Windcall cookbook.

Nonetheless, a few residents have turned the tables on Kay and her assistants by fixing ethnic or regional dishes and inviting the cooks for dinner. I remember a delicious competition between Kay's pumpkin pie and a Southern resident's sweet potato version. Everybody won.

Of course, there are those individuals who have some difficulty with the food. A few have admitted to going off to Bozeman to relieve their fast-food cravings at McDonald's or Taco John's! And one bought her own bag of instant mashed potatoes because she had long ago lost her taste for the real thing.

Yet even these renegades value the evening meal for another reason: it provides a reliable opportunity and a comfortable setting to gather together and talk. Most groups linger beyond dessert to share personal histories and discuss their work — or at least they do eventually.

While Albert and I had assumed that one of the main attractions of our program would be the residents' opportunity to spend time with each other, we were startled to learn that very few arrived with an expectation of that sort. Quite the contrary. Many admitted that they had felt uneasy about living with strangers who worked in their field. They expected rivalry rather than camaraderie.

The memory of an experience I had in the 1970s helped me understand the residents' uneasiness. A former therapy client had asked me to help her start a support group for directors of local nonprofits. Mary ran a program for at-risk teens in a community that had about a dozen other nonprofits serving the city and its residents. There was virtually no contact between the groups' leaders, and she hoped that if they met regularly, they could trade solutions to the many problems they all shared. She also suspected, however, that some difficult issues would come up first: all of the organizations had to compete for a piece of the same funding pie, so there was a history of suspicion and competition. Mary wanted me there while the group explored the tensions and fears that kept them sequestered from support they might give each other.

Many of our residents seemed to feel a similar isolation. John Musick's long history of working for social justice began with his efforts to register black voters in Alabama during the civil rights movement. Now he directs an organizing project in low-income communities in Michigan where changing demographics have sparked racial tensions. At first John was worried about sharing two weeks with other organizers and activists.

So much of our world, both inside and outside of organizing, is competitive. We learn to live by our wits, knowing that even those we broadly call colleagues are often competitors for recognition, respect, and especially money. Accordingly, how successful could I expect an organizers' retreat to be?

Karen Fant later expressed a similar pessimism on a more personal level. Reading the biographies sent out prior to the start of each session, she noticed that nobody else in her group was working on environmental issues. She prepared herself to feel isolated and disconnected from her housemates.

Neither John nor Karen was ready for what actually happened. John was profoundly moved and encouraged by his group's easy coalescence. He found that instead of stirring competition, their similar work experiences became a unifying force.

Karen wrote that she would remember her residency as a special experience shared with very special people.

> A time when I could talk and listen, when I could understand and
> be understood, when I could reach out and know that I was supported.
> In the sharing and grieving, in the helping each other, we were helped
> deeply ourselves. And we left stronger, more balanced and centered,
> and more ready to resume our lives anew.

Albert and I have noticed that the residents who come to us from faith-based organizations seem a little different than the others. They might be just as weary, but most don't seem to feel as isolated or as emotionally drained. Instead, they carry a sturdy sense of knowing that they belong to a team. They tell us that staff members meet frequently to check in with one another. Several emphasize the important role that mentors played in their training and then later as advisors. Because of their common religious roots, I expect as well that these organizations better understand the commitment to living their values. They have a language with which to talk about it and rituals that affirm it.

My therapy office had provided a safe arena for Mary and her group to address the mutual fears that had blocked their collaboration. Through dialogue, they were able to replace suspicions with firsthand knowledge of one another. Eventually they jumped into discussions about the personal cost of nonprofit work and shared ways of coping.

Windcall offers residents an equally effective way to reach the same goal. Instead of competing for dollars, they make breakfast together, risk a group horseback ride, or laugh about their childlike works of art. They share experiences that make it easy to discover and embrace their deeper connections: the common ground they share in their individual journeys and their sustaining values, goals, and dreams.

For some residents, Windcall also is their first chance to have meaningful conversations with social justice workers outside their own issue area and their own region. They compare their different challenges and approaches and learn from each other. Most are grateful to be reminded of the wide and committed network to which they belong.

Not surprisingly, just beneath their caution, some find a hunger that also propels them toward connection with their housemates. Given the intense pace of their work, few have much time or energy for friends. For many, it has been a long time since they have lingered over dinner or sat around the living room and indulged in unhurried personal exchanges. During their weeks at Windcall, residents have the chance to rediscover the pleasure of making friends. They also discover that similar objectives and struggles provide a trustworthy structure for honest communication.

All of the residents probably find safety in the fact that they are relative strangers placed together in an environment that is new to everyone. They share no personal past or assured future. They have little to lose and much to learn by being open and risking meaningful exchanges. Their adventure together often includes an unusual degree of self-revelation and intimacy.

Carl Anthony is an accessible, big-hearted man with an easy smile. As director of the Urban Habitat Program in San Francisco, he used his background in architecture and urban planning to nurture and promote multicultural urban environmental leadership. At Windcall he shared his time with three female residents. Carl captured the comfort and warmth that characterized his group when he wrote:

Then it rained. It rained for days and we made a fire and sang songs
from the sixties. It was like we had known each other a long time ago
and had been separated for years and now we were getting together to
find out what had happened during the time we had been apart.

Carl and his group deepened their friendships in the guesthouse while
snugly barricaded against the elements. Other resident groups come together
venturing to Yellowstone. In our early years of operation, we would merely
suggest such a trip. But once we saw how it affected the relationships in each
foursome, we began to actively promote it.

Days before their trip, residents clear the dinner table, spread out maps
of the park, and refer to Albert's dog-eared "Yellowstone in a Day" itinerary.
They read brochures and notes from their predecessors about previous excursions and spend hours planning the perfect route. Almost none of them have
been to the park before. When they finally see the steaming pools and ther-
mal eruptions, the Grand Canyon of the Yellowstone River, the herds of bison
and elk, and, if they're lucky, a grizzly or wolf, their shared excitement
cements a memory and bond they are unlikely to forget.

On a smaller scale, residents sometimes go into town to listen to live
music or visit the Museum of the Rockies. Sharing a long ride up the mountain on horseback and the resulting sore muscles can definitely strengthen a
sense of community. Much in the same way, one group told us that they had
laughed so hard watching each other's efforts to throw a pot on the wheel that
they were bound forever by the secret of their shared ineptitude.

Laughter is a powerful bonding agent. It is also a strong antidote to
heavy responsibility. Yet it is most often generated by free time spent in good
company, and too few of our hard-working residents make much room for
recreational time with friends. It is not surprising, therefore, that many of
them find and treasure the fun they have with their Windcall cohorts.

Tema Okun grew up in North Carolina during the civil rights movement.
When she applied to Windcall in 1991, she was assisting a wide range of
grassroots and nonprofit organizations in the South through organizational
assessment and training. In her application she described both her deep and
abiding commitment to social and economic justice and the physical and

emotional exhaustion that she was feeling. She spoke movingly about what she hungered to find during her residency.

I want to be in touch with that part of me and that part of the world that is creative and loving and full of energy. I want to struggle with joy, not despair.

Thanks to her housemates, Tema got her wish. At the end of her weeks at Windcall she wrote:

I have laughed in my belly, laughed at a look, laughed for no reason at all. Noisily and with gusto. I now know the meaning of the word guffaw. I have been guffawing.

Vivian Chang spent her formative political years addressing the same oppressive working conditions in Oakland, California, that her grandmother, a garment worker in the sweatshops of Taiwan, had experienced fifty years before. Ten years after Tema's residency, Vivian echoed her feelings about the healing power of laughter shared with new friends.

I applied to Windcall wanting to sit down somewhere quiet, have time to read, and just to be alone. Boy, I had no idea I would be laughing so hard that my stomach ached, bantering away on hikes, and giggling about horse flatulence as we rode up the trail.

Since residents are placed at Windcall solely on the basis of their requested dates, we make no effort to manage the makeup of each group. We never know what each composite personality will turn out to be. Some four-somes are characteristically independent — each member going in his or her own chosen direction — while other groups seem joined at the hip.

For the latter, the company of their fellow residents becomes a primary catalyst for renewal, even if the importance of their new friendships often comes as a surprise. Vivian Chang's group was made up of Scott Douglas, the executive director of a metropolitan, interfaith, interracial organization in Alabama; Stephanie Gut, who runs a grassroots community organization representing 41,000 families in San Diego; and Chris Ho, a senior staff attorney for a public interest law practice in San Francisco.

This group wrote a joint *Impression*. In it they revealed their astonishment at the great chemistry that quickly developed between them. They marveled that four strangers who came of political age at different times in different racial communities could become such fast friends. Their bonding seemed all the more miraculous because three of them admitted that on arrival they had no expectations of even liking those unknown others with whom they would be randomly thrown together.

> It was amazing that those of us who came here feeling exhausted, ugly, burned out, and even positively antisocial were renewed, energized, and inspired by our companionship and found even our enforced routine of the six o'clock dinnertime strangely comforting.

These bonds of friendship may endure far beyond Windcall. One group found that they had very different areas of expertise even within their common field of work. They helped each other professionally during their residency and then continued with frequent phone consultations long after they left. Another close-knit foursome of women was determined to keep their relationships intact. They traveled from four different states to spend a week together several times after their 1993 residency. In 1997 we received a note from Greenport, Long Island, where they were enjoying another reunion.

> Our experience at Windcall fostered a lasting friendship that continues to support and sustain us and the Windcall protocols i.e. taking care of yourself, having the luxury of time and space, linger with us over these years. We share good talk and our deepening friendships give us much help with life's passages.
> *Love from Sue Jones, Lois Barber, Joyce Dukes, and Jackie Lynn*

Walter Davis coordinates the training and technical assistance program that the Tennessee Southern Empowerment Project provides to other nonprofits in the region. In 1998 he was one of a rare all-male Windcall resident group. At a Jobs for Justice conference recently, he was unexpectedly tackled by one of his mates. Walter told us:

> I hear this yell. Someone grabs me and twirls me around in the hall-way. It is like we have known each other for decades. Our residency was an intense bonding experience.

Each year there are a couple of groups who tell us with great satisfaction that theirs is the most amazing combination of residents ever to inhabit the guesthouse. Some are quite sure that we are responsible for their good luck and want to know how we decided to put them together. Unfortunately, we can't claim the credit, but such declarations do give us enormous pleasure. We know that what our residents are really extolling is the unexpected gift of relationship.

The tales we hear about mealtime in the guesthouse remind me of the ancient and powerful ritual of breaking bread together. In this tradition, which is part of many cultures, individuals share food and stories and embrace their common humanity. Around the dinner table, residents rediscover and savor the sustenance of community. They also experience one of the great benefits of friendship: the restorative power of laughter.

I have been inspired by the essential beauty of wilderness, of a genuine silence, of a comforting darkness, but even more by the deep compassion and sense of humanity of my fellow residents. They reflect what is best in us—compassion, dedication and an unambiguous balance between intolerance of oppression and love for common folk. Windcall allows us to surround ourselves not only with trees, flowers, birds, and streams—but with the deep-rooted strength of freedom fighters.

—*Bill Gallegos (1995)*

Windcall 10/4/02

The best part was the people.

No. The best part was the silence.

Or the hikes with Jesse.

Or throwing pots, running my hands over the earthen, slippery clay.

Or the food, and someone else's cooking.

Or time to write.

Or the snow dusting the mountains.

No! The best part was the dinnertime conversations with passionate committed coconspirators.

Or the fires in the woodstove at night, lolling on the couches, reading in silent companionship.

Or Kay's chocolate chip cookies.

Or riding Doc, the beautiful Appaloosa.

No! The best part was being touched by the spirits of all the residents come before, their work, their passion, their words and images, that fill this wondrous space.

Or the sunsets from the hill every night after dinner.

Or the snow falling silently as stars.

Or the wind whispering in the trees.

No. It's the camaraderie.

No. It's the solitude.

No. The best part was driving with new friends through the Lamar Valley of Yellowstone watching big, wooly-headed bison cross the road.

Or climbing the ridge to the bare knob above Windcall, looking down on the green and gold patchwork miles of the Gallatin Valley and the toy houses of our magical refuge below, and the black and white dots of cows and horses, surrounded by purple mountains, Jesse by my side, magpies gliding by, distant train and hum of interstate and airport, people going somewhere, and me, still as can be.

No! The best part was our passionate last night discussion over chocolate cake around the fire about the role of spirituality in our work and our lives, talking close to midnight though none of us had packed, not wanting to stop our eager absorption of each other's wisdom.

And now that everyone is gone but me and I rattle around the hollow rooms of the studio barn writing this, I know, yes, the best part was the people.

—*Francis Reid*

With the unanimous accord of Leonardo Vilchis,
Michelann Bewsee, and Miriam Brown (2002)

10 Nature and the Land

*I'm not a painter, but if I were I would sit down at the pond
until I learned how to mix dragonfly blue. I would walk these
paths and stare at the goldenrod until I could see anew and
match the pigment. I would capture on canvas the spread
and slope of this blessed valley, the cragginess of Ross and
the gentle dip of its saddle, the purple shadows of the
infoldings of rock. I would memorize the brilliant flash
of the western tanager and the grace of the great blue
heron—the straight stretch of her legs toward water, the
gentle curve of her neck toward sky.*

—Linda Burnham (1992)

*n*ature in the Rockies can be astonishing, dramatic, and difficult to
ignore: thunder ricocheting off the mountains, lightning fracturing
the sky, a chorus of coyotes shattering the night silence. And it can present a
panorama of equally amazing soft moments: wisps of morning fog forming
and drifting up against the mountains, the fresh smell of rain coming up from
the valley, sunlight polishing wet clusters of orange mountain ash berries, a
sudden breeze launching hundreds of thistle seeds into the clear autumn sky.

No single element in the Windcall program has a more powerful effect
on the residents than the physical place itself. The beauty, surprise, and
authority of nature stir each individual. Those who live and labor in urban

areas find the landscape and its inhabitants wild and amazing. Even rural residents are awed by the grandeur of the fabled American West.

At first, some are cautious and even fearful of nature's scale and drama, but sooner or later all are drawn to make tentative explorations. Ted Bryan capitalizes on those beginning steps and leads residents through country he knows intimately. Under his guidance a trail ride becomes a chance to discover all that the forest and fields reveal.

Seen through Ted's eyes, the land presents fascinating stories: tree stumps pulled apart by ant-hungry bears or chokecherry branches broken by their lust for ripening berries. A young lodgepole pine, its bark hanging in strips, tells of an elk who rubbed the velvet from his antlers. A fresh hole made in a dying aspen reveals a fine, new home for a family of sapsuckers.

Many residents marvel at the incredible variety of life around them: twenty different kinds of grasses, fifty-six kinds of wildflowers, and sixty-four recorded species of birds on the Windcall property alone. Alexa Bradley, who painted numerous versions of the Montana sky, also kept a diary that chronicled her daily discoveries.

> Pine siskin, Cassin's finch, evening grosbeak, lazuli bunting, meadowlark, mountain bluebird . . . fairy slipper, larkspur, forget-me-not, wild rose, sticky geranium . . . this is the natural history of my day.
>
> I am becoming wild here. Wild like the land. I bike down gravel roads collecting dry grass, sagebrush, one of every wildflower I can find, feathers, rocks, pieces of wood. I suppose I am trying to incorporate this place into my bones and blood.

Some residents muse on the opposites they find in nature: constant change alongside mountains that have changed little throughout the centuries. Naomi Swinton, who organizes against the privatization of prisons in the South, was awed by the juxtaposition of life and death that she saw daily.

> Everywhere I look there is abundance — grasses, trees, animals, mountains, creeks; and everywhere there is also evidence of dying and death. The dry grasses bent, tree trunks returned to earth, carcasses, bones, dry open plains, and a cold wind to match the sun.

Jackie Kittrell felt intoxicated by the land and concluded that she had seriously underestimated the importance of having such beauty in her life. In her own state of Tennessee, the Smokey Mountains were not that far away from where she lived, yet she had never thought to go there.

A self-proclaimed "suited, nylon-wearing briefcase attorney" and a mother of three wild boys, Jackie counsels and represents nuclear-weapons-plant workers in Oak Ridge. People in that community, where the bomb dropped on Hiroshima was made, endure a legacy of health problems from exposure to radioactive materials. Jackie carries the weight of their tragic stories. She left Windcall awakened to the way nature soothed her and lightened that burden, and she vowed to seek the healing of her own mountains.

When I came to Windcall, the land also stopped me in my tracks. In California I had been juggling a family, graduate school, and then a private practice; this required years of careful planning and judicious use of time. Yet I seemed always in a rush to get to my next appointment and even used my rare time off as a chance to prepare for the next challenge. Then I closed my practice, moved to Montana for an entire summer, and felt that I had dropped into a still, lush, and astounding place. That place could be found on a map, but it also felt like forgotten territory inside.

Thinking of my own first months at Windcall reminds me of a quotation I have kept in my desk for over twenty-five years. "A man is finally defined by what he does with his attention," wrote poet John Ciardi. When I first read this statement, it jolted and intrigued me. It was so like a poem by Walter de la Mare that was a favorite when our children were little.

It's a very odd thing —
As odd as can be —
That whatever Miss T. eats
Turns into Miss T.

Was it that simple, that what I choose and attend to forms me? I had always figured things the other way around: who I am determines what I will do. These lines came back to help me understand an important part of Windcall's impact on me and on the residents who followed.

As I did that first year and still do each time I return, many residents feel a shift in their behavior as they spend unaccustomed periods of time attending to nature. They gradually let go of their predominant reliance on reason and action and instead find themselves standing still in the moment, perceiving the world through their senses and responding to it with spontaneity and a flood of feeling. Emotion gives life vibrancy and meaning. Feeling deeply is synonymous with being alive. The land has the power to transform residents' habitual focus on *doing* into an exhilarated state of just *being*.

Tula Jaffe, for example, was startled by her own behavior. All her adult life she has been a relentless activist for social justice. According to her associates, Tula was fierce and formidable when it came to confronting any inequity in her community. One afternoon as she worked in the studio barn, she glanced out the window and saw three jet-black horses with fresh snow on their backs. She stopped writing mid-sentence, left her desk, grabbed her coat, and climbed over the pasture fence to pet them. Tula recalled:

> Not only that, one allowed me to put my face right up against the soft
> side of his cheek, where I let it stay for a few seconds and smelled his
> sweet, earthy, horsey essence. I returned to the porch of the studio,
> looked back at the horses, and cried without trying to figure out why.

Reading her words, I think I understand Tula's tears. I, too, have been unexpectedly jerked into the present by some compelling natural beauty. In that instant I don't weigh or analyze. I simply follow my desire to share in whatever small miracle I perceive. Free of confusion, I move from my heart with joy, a feeling of gratitude, and almost always with tears.

Our residents have few openings in their busy lives for such moments of awe. Yet nourishment for tired souls is often found in just such an instant, when we are lifted out of the quagmire of our individual concerns and transported to a grateful recognition of the gift of life. Residents experience the power of wonder and relearn that if they make time for it, nature can offer this renewal anytime, anywhere.

I find repeated affirmation of Ciardi's words in the transformation that nature brings about in the residents. As their attention is captured by mountain vistas, fields of wildflowers, or simply the beauty of the sky in all its moods, residents visibly change into someone new — or perhaps just forgotten. They become childlike: instinctive, unrestrained, and joyful. They become artists and poets and writers expressing what has stirred their emotions or given them new hope.

After her intense period of mourning for friends lost to AIDS, Kay Whitlock was stirred by the land and opened to a new depth of feeling about life.

> I have been filled with joy here in moments when I've gone outside to look at stars in the deep darkness of the night sky and when I've seen a line of elk moving together across a field. Laughter bubbled up inside of me with the feel of wind in my hair. The moments when I am outside seem to be moments of prayer and the prayer is this: Thank you. Thank you for the chance to simply be alive and to be part of all this: the work, yes, and the land.

During my childhood years of constantly moving households, it was the land that sheltered me and provided continuity. The houses and apartments we rented held other people's furniture, preferences, and dreams. We perched there with only a few of our own possessions. I remember feeling most at home outdoors — playing in a stream that ran in the gully below one house, climbing on the rocky shore of a reservoir not far from another, and hiding away in the branches of many good climbing trees.

Jose Montenegro left his native Mexico to come to the United States fourteen years before coming to Windcall. He makes his home in the Salinas Valley of California, but his work organizing and training forestry workers took him to the Pacific Northwest. At dinner with us during the last week of his residency, he told us that living at Windcall was the first time he had truly felt at home in this country. In a pencil drawing, Jose expressed his sense of homecoming. The familiar profile of the nearby Bridgers dominates, but a closer look reveals that the mountains are formed by the curved and jutted shapes of Aztec Indians. In Windcall's natural setting, so like the region where he grew up, Jose felt the comforting presence of his ancestors.

Janet Robideau is a member of the Northern Cheyenne tribe and knows well her people's important link to the earth. Even so, she too had lost that connection in the heat of her efforts for social justice.

> I remember my Grandpa telling us that we needed to stop and listen when Mother Earth speaks to us. Over the years, I haven't listened as closely as I could have, should have. I've been too busy working, fighting, urging, prodding, pushing, encouraging, winning, losing, etc. I'd forgotten what it is like to just sit and experience her great beauty. I'd forgotten what it is like to feel her breath on my cheek and to reach out and run my fingers through her hair. I'd forgotten the feel of her skin on my bare feet.

Perhaps most importantly, the residents' encounters with nature and the land can trigger a critical change in the way they approach their work. Many arrive at Windcall anxious and burdened with responsibilities. They witness the dire effects of social inequities on people for whom change comes far too slowly. They live in the urgency of need, even though they know that progress takes years to achieve. They feel that they can never do enough and that time is running out.

Here, residents live in the shadow of mountains that have been around for thousands of years. They sit beside two-hundred-year-old fir trees and cross streams that had cut a path down to the valley long before they were born. Living in the midst of such longevity helps them begin to see their own lives and goals in a different perspective. They experience a sense of belonging, of having a modest yet irreplaceable role to play in the larger scheme of things. They begin to feel part of a cumulative contribution in a long and important struggle.

Vickie Smedley works on environmental issues in Pennsylvania, but it was at Windcall one night that she felt the larger truth about her place in nature and recognized the underlying point of all her efforts.

> We sat on the bluff waiting for the elk herd to appear and watching the sunset. A light steady rain started. We huddled together in the high grass under a poncho, watching. The sunlight behind the rain made it look like threads of a silvery cobweb connecting the sky and the earth.

Sitting there I felt my own connection to nature and to my ancestors, my children and my grandchildren to come. I knew in that moment that these connections are the reason I do the work I do, so that I may honor that which is most important — life itself.

Nature provides many with new spiritual ground on which to stand, a place in which they are neither the linchpin of the struggle nor insignificant to it. This perspective strengthens a commitment that is both enduring and more humanely paced. Residents receive a healing affirmation that allows for a balance between their own well-being and their passionate work to protect the rights of others. They feel their link to an ongoing human journey.

One morning I got up early to walk down the Roller Coaster Road and found the entire valley below hung with rainbows. They were falling out of the clouds, the morning light suddenly visible in all of its colors, transformed. I had found my image for Windcall. Like a prism, it makes the lives that pass through it visible in new ways. It transforms them.

—Karen Lehman (1996)

11 The House on the Hill

Windcall will always be a treasured and unforgettable experi-
ence for me. And part of that was knowing I was welcome in
your home and that you folks would come down to the guest-
house for dinner and share your world with us.

—*Robert Bray (1996)*

Straight up the hill from the guesthouse is our home. About seventy-five yards of gravel path skirt some chokecherry bushes and small aspens to connect the two buildings. The houses are so close that on summer evenings we often can hear laughter drifting up from the residents' porch. At bedtime, if Jesse is still waiting hopefully for one last walker to emerge from the guesthouse, we call him home easily with a whistle or two. In the early years of the resident program, the distance between the guesthouse and our house on the hill seemed much greater. Then, things changed.

At first I didn't expect to be very involved with the residents. I thought of Windcall as Albert's project. He was the one who had wanted to create a conference center and who had been so dispirited when the idea wasn't feasible. I came up with the resident program only in order to salvage some of his dream.

In the conference center scenario, I wouldn't have had any ongoing role.

Once it was up and running, even Albert's participation would be ancillary. We both carried these expectations into the new project. We saw ourselves becoming rather like the host and hostess of a good bed-and-breakfast. We would play an essential but behind-the-scenes part by putting together a warm and inviting environment and removing as much responsibility from the residents as we could. We would see to it that things ran smoothly. Then we would get out of the way.

We assumed that with their needs taken care of by the staff, residents would want to get to know their peers or spend time on their own. Once we had greeted newcomers and oriented them to the ranch, further personal involvement on our part could even prove burdensome. Some of our guests might feel an awkward obligation to engage with us and no one wants to spend their vacation taking care of the innkeepers.

During the first few years, however, several things happened that began to change our point of view. One morning as I went out for a run, I met a new resident starting out on a similar trip. Twenty-seven-year-old Arturo Vargas had applied to the program for time to catch up with himself. As a young, well-educated Latino man devoted to social change, the pressure on him to assume a position of leadership in his community was intense. He wanted a chance to think and make sure that he didn't move too fast and get in over his head.

Arturo and I jogged for several miles together. As we chatted, he chuckled and told me that he and his fellow residents had had a rather funny conversation the night before. Each had shared his or her fantasy about Albert's and my real reasons for providing them with such a grand opportunity. Their imaginings were very creative. In the one I remember, eventually we would show up at their door in gold robes to recruit the newcomers for an extremist religious sect.

I knew their scenarios were invented in jest, but the therapist in me noticed that they also held an important message. The residents were imagining our intentions because they had no way of knowing what they really were. By standing apart we had unwittingly encouraged them to see us only as mysterious benefactors who lived in the house on the hill. It was our land, our program, our personal funds. We couldn't hide from those truths and all they might imply to our guests. Of course the residents would wonder about us, and lacking real contact, they would make their own assumptions and projections.

Because most of them lived and worked in poor communities, many struggled to feel comfortable with the comparative luxury here. Some also faced the adjustment of being a person of color in a very white region. We too had our unsettling moments. I remember one resident who arrived wearing a T-shirt that proclaimed "Bankers Are the Bandits!" He had been campaigning in his community to make lending rates less discriminatory against low-income people. Forgetting that momentarily, I got caught up in the disquieting possibility that he saw us that way as well.

It occurred to me that keeping our distance might undermine some of the comfort and safety we had worked so hard to create. If we wanted to set our guests at ease with us and vice versa, we needed to recognize the inevitable socioeconomic and racial barriers that would exist and find ways to lessen them. The best way I knew to do that was to show ourselves as individuals, each with our own untidy mix of human strengths and foibles. We needed to find an appropriate level of regular interaction with the residents and play a more personal role in the program.

Something else was also gradually eroding our decision to stay out of the way. The residents were interesting, intelligent individuals who shared our values and were doing amazing work. We often had acquaintances in common from our years of supporting organizations like theirs through Abelard. Some had even been Abelard grantees themselves. In addition, every foursome had been a unique and intriguing composite personality. We found ourselves looking forward to meeting arrivals and discovering the flavor of each new group.

But there was an even larger factor that encouraged me to expand my involvement. I had begun to notice what the residents actually were doing with their time. They were not just resting here. Each one had begun a unique process of restoring something of personal value that had been shoved aside or lost to overwork.

Suddenly I realized I was on home turf. This was not just Albert's passion for which I had created a new container. With less intention than I like to admit, I had carved out a project with a scale and purpose that fit me perfectly. I had spent over fifteen years helping individuals heal and make positive changes in their lives. While no direct therapy would take place at Windcall, I could certainly use my training to ensure that the program not only promoted rest and renewal, but also supported reflection and experimentation.

I began to think about my years as a therapist. All the clients I had worked with carried within them an innate impulse toward health and well-being. That is what brought them to my door. Whether specifically expressed or not, they knew something in their lives was not working on their own behalf anymore. My job was to nourish that positive thrust toward change and help my clients recognize and challenge whatever blocked its path. Our time together provided a safe place for them to discover new perspectives and ways of being.

In the resident program, I recognized some similarities. Our guests were here in hopes of finding some kind of renewal and revitalization. Most were dealing with symptoms that were beginning to limit their effectiveness at work and the quality of their lives in general. They were working to understand the causes of their distress and, like my former clients, they were seeking a safe place and time to be constructively self-centered. How could we provide that place and also be instrumental in helping them reconnect with their own internal healing resources?

I started to see that we had to be far more than custodians of the Windcall program. Many of our residents would struggle with hard issues here. If we expected them to take risks, we needed to become a visible and accessible part of a supportive environment.

Perhaps of greatest importance, Albert and I could, like the therapist, align ourselves with our residents' desire to be whole and healthy. We could be sensitive to their processes and notice moments when we might help them along. We could throw our weight behind their explorations and encourage them to rediscover and repair their own inner compasses.

Over the years we have learned other details of our job description from the residents themselves. For one thing, they have taught us that most, regardless of age, see us as parental figures. Tula Jaffe, the resident who had leapt from her desk to nuzzle a snow-covered horse, wrote:

> As their child for two weeks, I experienced an enhanced sense of self-esteem. All children need to feel that they are as special to their parents as the Wellses made us feel when they told us we were their heroes. I will be sixty-four on my next birthday and I wonder if it is too late to be adopted!

That particular revelation reminded us that our words carry a lot of weight. Again, like the therapist, we are granted an elevated level of authority because of our position as hosts.

All these feelings and insights began to pile up and lead us to increase our involvement in the program. We lengthened the orientation session and we let residents know that we would enjoy joining them one night for dinner. When our paths crossed, we lingered to talk.

Now we know, as well, the power of small deeds. Each time we fix something at the guesthouse, deliver mail, take pictures of residents riding or throwing a pot — do any small task for them — we are underscoring our respect and regard for them. We have learned to accept the stature we are granted and the responsibility we have to use it mindfully.

Of course we must still find the right balance — different from group to group — between protecting our residents' time to themselves and participating in their experience. Whatever time we do spend with them has steadily become more personal and disclosing. Most want to hear the story of our own meandering journey to the Windcall Resident Program. Many also ask what we have learned from them. We use such questions as an opening to discuss with increasing candor the consequences of habitual overwork and share all that we have discovered about burnout's insidious progression and how it can be disrupted.

As expected, the mutual level of comfort has risen in direct proportion to our visibility and transparency. We no longer have to read their *Impressions* to find out what residents discover here. We simply ask them. Over time, we have become part of the residents' learning experience and in return, they also have become more directly part of ours. We often consult them when we are making decisions about improving elements of the program or when we are trying to solve a problem. They are important advisors.

In about our third year, for example, my enthusiastic husband thought the program was doing so well that he wanted to add on to the guesthouse and double the size of the groups. Not surprisingly, I strongly disagreed. We decided to resolve our stalemate by asking participants in each session that year to comment on the idea. Much to my relief, they unanimously vetoed expansion and extolled the advantages of retaining an intimate atmosphere. They cited the ease with which four people could get to know each other and do things together, yet spend time alone as well. We followed their advice while joking privately about how handy it would be to bring all of our differences of opinion down the hill for review.

Next we decided to experiment with allowing couples to attend Windcall as long as each applicant had been accepted on his or her own merits. There was one guesthouse bedroom larger than the others that easily could accommodate two people. We were concerned, however, that if the twosome ignored their housemates and spent most of their time together, they would disrupt the comfortable group dynamic. After a few trial runs, we gathered feedback. Our guests told us that our fears were unfounded. The couples didn't spend a majority of their time apart from the others. They equally valued opportunities to be with their new friends, together and alone.

During our first eight years we witnessed a huge growth in use of the Internet. How should access to the residents' one phone line for email and calls home be regulated? Our guests' responses were adamant, ranging from suggestions to remove computers altogether to adding new phone lines. After we discussed it with several different groups, however, one came up with a wise but simple solution. We should mention the problem during the orientation and ask each foursome to work it out among themselves. We agreed.

Over time, residents also have become our primary source for contacting and supporting applicants. Since they have been here themselves, they recognize which of their cohorts will make the best use of the program. They know, as well, how to address the fears that keep many from applying.

Increasingly, the residents are our partners in the effort to make Windcall an important refuge for those who work for social, economic, and environmental justice. Since 1992 former residents have served on the selection committee, in recent years holding half of the eight positions. The second one to join us was the man who wore the disconcerting T-shirt. This wise, kind person got a good laugh when I told him how intimidating he had seemed.

In 2001 a group of eight former residents came together to envision how the Windcall idea and intent might continue beyond the time when Albert and I would end our stewardship. Their goal was to research possible alternatives for housing and funding a permanent program that followed the Windcall model. They also sought to define and describe the basic elements that made the existing program effective and worth replicating.

To accomplish the latter they spent their first evening together reminiscing and sharing. Each spoke at length about his or her own resident experience and what had contributed to the transformative value of their stay. From that long and personal conversation they constructed a statement of mission that spoke of building and sustaining social justice movement leadership through the essential supports they had found at Windcall. They listed the opportunities for individual reflection and unstructured time, for creative expression and exploration, for healing from external and internalized oppression, and for time to experience the beauty, power, and wisdom of the natural environment.

Two years later, a second group of seasoned social justice leaders stepped in to spearhead the next stage of the process. Their task was to discover and develop a specific site and other methods for sustaining leadership.

Now, as some others have done at Windcall, Albert and I have begun the process of letting go of a project that we have tended with our energies and hearts for many years. It is not an easy task. We will deeply miss all the excitement and pleasure it has given to our lives. Most of all we will miss the amazing people it has brought to our door. We have great trust, however, in those who are taking responsibility for keeping the essence of the program alive. We are moved by the work and commitment of these extremely busy individuals.

Both Albert and I have been greatly rewarded by what began as a replacement for a lost dream. We have been pushed by our experiment to weave together our different skills and interests so we could express our thanks to the organizers and activists we so admire. Now the very people we sought to honor are honoring us in turn by seeking to keep the values and goals of Windcall alive. We could receive no finer affirmation.

When Windcall was founded in 1989, it was the only place in the country where social justice organizers and activists could go for unstructured time to reflect. Today, it is still the only retreat program that neither prescribes nor demands, but simply trusts that movement leaders will discover what it is they need from the experience. Windcall's impact has been profound, for individuals, for organizations, and for the broader movement.

—*The Windcall Futures Project Mission Statement and Funding Proposal (2003)*

Prayer (excerpt)

before you begin
whatever you surely
are beginning here

say a prayer for windcall,
a temple to the sacredness of our work
our spiritual assistance center
the soul's clearinghouse

breathe a prayer deep for its creators
who offer silence and oil paints
coyotes and computers
bears and freedom
freedomfreedomfreedom.

—*Sandra Jerabek (1994)*

12 The Big Barn

What I want to say to future residents boils down to this: whatever your bent, jump into it here! This place aims to help you find out what you need and get some of it. The world should be a place where everyone is so lucky. I guess that is how we got into this work we do.

—Jan Adams (2001)

*t*he big barn was built in 1913 from trees felled on the property and taken to the local mill across the valley. When we took ownership in 1986, its stone foundation showed the results of decades of pressure from the earth on its uphill side. It had been pushed inward toward the west, causing the barn to list almost eighteen degrees off center in the opposite direction. Sunlight and swallows entered at will through broken windows and holes in the roof. But it was this beautiful old building that had first drawn Albert to the site and we didn't want to lose it.

Our contractor warned that the winds and snow loads of one more heavy winter would probably bring the structure down, so we decided on a risky undertaking. We would pour a new foundation where the old one had once stood and then attempt to lift and straighten the barn before repositioning it on that sturdier base. One fall morning three carpenters ran steel cables along the structure's east and west sides for support and put eight come-along jacks in place. Then, after carefully removing all the old exterior siding so that the remaining skeleton would have greater flexibility, slowly and painstakingly they began to jack the building into vertical alignment. Five cranks on each of the west-side jacks were answered by backing off five cranks on their east-side counterparts.

We held our breath as the structure began to shift inch by inch. Old timbers groaned and creaked and we knew that because of its age, the barn was as likely to collapse as to straighten. But straighten it did. Albert, the architect, the contractor, the carpenters, and I all cheered as the frame came to rest on its new foundation and stood strong and square again. It continued to stand tall as the carpenters added plywood sheathing, trusses, and beams, siding and roof, and some wide-paned windows reclaimed from a torn-down school-house. We placed four sets of these in the west wall to overlook the pond, the pastures, and the valley beyond and to catch the reflection of our legendary Montana sunsets.

This process of bringing the barn back into balance later became our metaphor for what the resident program is all about. Like that weathered building, people also can get knocked off center by sustained pressure. A friend's crisis, an illness, a passion, or even a valuable opportunity can pull us too far in one direction when we give all our energies to it. Ideally, once we have met that need, we bounce back — just like the children's plastic clown that when pushed over always returns to center. But sometimes we need assistance to rediscover that place of equilibrium.

While each resident comes to Windcall with an individual agenda, they also bring a shared one. All are carrying the effects of their intense and grueling work. They bear obvious signs of too much pressure withstood for too long and lives that are out of balance. These men and women have given Albert and me a front-row seat for observing the causes and symptoms of burnout. They also have shown us what can interrupt its course and reverse its damage.

Residents arrive in varying states of exhaustion. After a day or two of rest, some bounce back and go about their individual pursuits. But for many, catching up on sleep is not enough. These people may find it very hard to relax, even though they are bone tired. Some are swept into a personal vortex of stored sadness and pain. Others start their residency feeling fragile and anxious, particularly about how to function without work to structure their time. Many also show the results of neglected bodies and stress-related ailments.

It doesn't take long before residents exhibit signs of change. By the end of the first week, their behavior begins to shift; they even look different. Our cooks quip that we should take pictures of them on the first and last days of their stay to record the dramatic difference. They are right: in most, it is striking. We often have dinner with a new group soon after they arrive and then again just before they leave. In our first encounter the residents interact with caution and reserve. In the second we can see how the tension seems to have drained from their bodies. They walk with greater motion. Their faces have softened and become more expressive. They freely engage with each other and with us. And they laugh a whole lot more.

Early on, we thought we were merely seeing the effects of a good vacation on people who worked hard and long at a difficult job. As a few years went by, however, we received from some residents tales, both written and verbal, of experiences and insights that seemed out of proportion to the length of time they had spent here. As a retired therapist, I was skeptical about their claims. I knew it took my clients a good deal longer than two to four weeks to alter old, well-grooved patterns. But the extraordinary feedback continued. Some described their residency with words like "life-changing" and "transformative." These people were clearly saying that they had learned something at Windcall that had enabled them to make some significant changes in their lives. Finally, even I had to take them seriously and look more carefully at what was happening.

As we focused on what drew the residents' attention and fed their spirits at Windcall, we made some discoveries. When they had committed themselves to social justice work, they had given up much more than high salaries and regular vacations. The majority gradually had relinquished a significant number of outside activities, interests, and relationships. They also had developed a companion practice of overriding any physical, emotional, or mental distress signals that might get in the way of achieving their goals on schedule.

By eliminating so many of these non-work elements from their lives, residents cut themselves off from nourishing activities that could act as a counterweight to the wear and tear of the job. By ignoring crucial inner warnings, they failed to recognize the limits of their own endurance. We began to understand what made so many susceptible to wearing themselves out. They were stuck in a chronic imbalance of overwork and suffering a steady decline of resources that grew more and more difficult to reverse.

But at Windcall we watched as residents hungrily began to pursue new adventures, relationships, creative expression and periods of reflection. As we read their writings about newly awakened senses, saw them laugh and play with each other or mourn their losses, we knew they were regaining parts of themselves that they had forgotten even existed. They were reassembling a multifaceted picture of themselves. They also were regaining the intricate system of inner feedback that balances needs and goals and helps each of us chart a healthy course.

Just as removing the old siding and roof timbers from the barn allowed greater flexibility for change, coming here opened up the structure of the residents' lives. By abruptly uprooting them from their work and placing them in a strange environment, Albert and I had intervened more powerfully than we had imagined. We had put them in a setting that made business as usual impossible. Instead, it supported a change of course. They had to try something new. Once they got over that initial jolt, residents began to look at unexplored terrain both outside and in. They flexed forgotten muscles and started to reassess routine patterns of thinking and behaving. They started to see themselves differently.

As they tried new activities, residents began to ask provocative questions that had formerly been too risky to contemplate, questions such as: What are the things that refresh and reenergize me? Why are they missing from my life and what does their absence cost me? With these inquiries, whether posed in solitude or in company, the residents begin to explore self-care.

In this very unfamiliar setting, many of these organizers and activists begin to see that the way they work is not healthy. In the beginning, the chance to do work based on their values had offered enough reward for their efforts. But somewhere along the way, the reciprocity was lost. They began to sacrifice too much and run on empty too often. At Windcall this pattern is disrupted. Organizational crises and the desperate needs of others no longer define their days. Eventually residents step far enough out of the old structure to see its price tag and recognize that its most onerous by-product is a loss of self. Many begin to explore a healthier work ethic that includes their own growth and well-being. They search for a way to continue to do the work they love and make room for their whole selves as well.

Just as he was leaving Windcall, Dan Hirsch wrote about himself and other organizers:

> We too need the caress of birdsong and the wind through aspen; we too need the profound and gentle silence that is at the heart of nature; we too need the company of like-minded souls, the laughter of fellowship, the joys of normal life. Our task is to balance the two — diligent, faithful, and effective work on behalf of those who suffer and our own need to partake deeply of the richness of nature and human relationships that is at the core of that for which we fight.

Everything at Windcall is a potential messenger for this critical lesson. Some teachers are human — housemates, staff, and past residents — while others are creatures — Jesse, a quarter horse, or a confusion of birds at the feeder. Residents learn from experiences like walking in the dark or sitting alone by a stream, witnessing an explosive summer thunderstorm or watching the elk herd grazing quietly at dusk. Mountains, wildflowers, the ever-changing light — anything in nature can touch them and lead to new discovery and meaning.

While many organizers and activists relish the simple luxury of spending time alone, they also discover the benefits of being in good company. They feel relieved to break through the isolation they experience in their work.

Almost everyone finds something here that hooks into their internal agenda and becomes a catalyst for their self-motivated and self-generated education and renewal. As we have watched this process, we have realized that we can increase the impact of these resident journeys through the variety of experiences we make available and through our own active encouragement. We can jump-start residents' forgotten resources by finding intriguing ways to awaken their energy, curiosity, and sense of adventure.

Once they begin to explore, residents feel what works. As they laugh uproariously with housemates, they may remember how long fun and companionship have been missing in their lives. While they are writing a poem, they might hear an important creative voice that has been unintentionally silenced. They may reconnect to vital inner feedback long muffled by the constant clamor of external demands. They can remember that their own responses are trustworthy teachers.

Understanding this process helped us recognize that the residents who make the best use of Windcall have some desire for inner reflection already stirring. Personal timing and capacity for self-awareness play an important part in deepening the long-term value of their Windcall experience. We decided to probe more directly for that information in our application by asking what motivated each to apply. We now evaluate these two elements carefully as we strive to optimize the program's potential.

Still, years into the program, despite all we were discovering about the ways Windcall could most effectively repair the damage caused by burnout, we were left with one unanswered question. Why were a significant number of residents able to benefit so much in such a short time? The search for the answer to this question led me back to what I first learned as a parent, then reaffirmed as a therapist. It also returned me to the image of straightening the big barn.

We carefully had inched the structure into realignment and then strengthened it with additional supports. But critical to the barn's future was the solid new foundation on which it came to rest. The most surprising discovery that Albert and I have made about the Windcall Resident Program is the central role played by simple human caring. It is the foundation that supports our residents' willingness to take risks and be honest with themselves and that bolsters their potential and courage to change. It may also be Windcall's most valuable teacher.

All of us long to be seen and validated. So little in our society recognizes our striving for our finest selves that such moments of affirmation, when they come, are extremely powerful.

Windcall sends the residents a forceful message that they are respected, worthy, and valuable. It is spoken in the mere existence of the program and repeated in all its daily details. From the home-baked cookies waiting for them on the first day to the last packet of Windcall pictures mailed to them at home, residents receive concrete evidence of our regard. This affirmation empowers them to take seriously their own need and right to a full and balanced life.

In their kind of work, activists and organizers are called to engage with both their heads and their hearts. Along with the values they hold dear and strive to realize, many bring to their task a deep empathy that strengthens their work. Organizers attempting to empower a poor community can root their actions in a felt understanding of not just the community's needs, but its members' values, fears, and hopes as well. Yet there is also a potential danger with this depth of involvement. The combination of their own determination to make a difference and their ongoing immersion in the pain and needs of others can lead to physical and emotional exhaustion.

These workers for social justice must learn how to be passionate without allowing themselves to be consumed; to care for the task at hand but to care for themselves, as well, every day. In order to do this, organizers and activists must be alive to their bodies and feelings so they can recognize when they begin to lose their balance. They must carry a strong sense of their own worth and a ready knowledge of the tools and actions that will help them return to center.

To that end, we have shaped the Windcall program to promote self-discovery and learning through experiences that engage the residents' bodies, emotions, and senses, as well as their minds. We trust that if they are held in a safe, supportive, and caring environment, they will reconnect with and strengthen their own innate capacity for self-healing. They will leave better equipped to bring their passion for work and their personal needs into a healthier balance. That equilibrium will protect them from burnout and hopefully, like our barn, they will stand strong and solid for many years to come.

Investing in people, trusting in us, surrounding us with many kinds of support— yields surprises. Taking away expectations is a way of freeing us to pay attention to different things, important things, things outside everyday frameworks, down unexpected paths. Windcall helps us not just to think outside the box, but to be outside the box. This is a very profound way to support growth, change and development.

—Debora Kodish (2005)

In

The goldfinch hammering at my window wants
In. Flowering lupine
Has put him in a jealous rage. It's everywhere:
A purple summons to the breeding grounds.
The bull breaks free from his pen.
The stag leans over the water, admiring his velvet.
The water is laced with testosterone.
The wind is fortified with pollen.
The bee gets drunk.
The goldfinch rises and beats his breast against the glass.

Wheel turning.
Clay rises in my hands.
I press down and it pushes back.
Faced with brute force of will, the clay shrugs.
I enter with my fingers, probing for the center, but the center will not hold.
Things fall apart
Again.

Begin again.
Cone up and press down.
Cone up
Press down.
Muscle tension. Water rolling down my arms.
Molecules align with a firm hand, but nothing emerges without a yielding heart.

The clay will decide.
I listen with my fingertips.
The goldfinch hovers at the window, flickering flame.
Together we wait.

—*Andy Robinson (2005)*

13 Bringing the Mountain Home

Carrying this place to Boston, planting and rooting the sensations and vast spiritual support of Windcall in my daily life at home will be my task. I am not sure if it will be possible in the boxed and paved conditions of urban living, but I had all but abandoned the possibility of anything like that when I boarded the plane that brought me here.

—Judith Robinson (2003)

*i*f you look to the northeast from almost anyplace at Windcall, the craggy shape of Ross Peak dominates the view. Many residents dream of climbing to its top, but only a very few complete the seven-hour ascent. Most of us are content to watch the light and cloud formations change hourly on the majestic peak, a less rigorous but still satisfying experience. For many organizers and activists, this mountain is the symbol of Windcall. It is the quiet, enduring sentinel that stands guard as they heal and rediscover themselves.

As a group nears the end of its stay, it is not uncommon for its members to regale us at dinner one evening with their fantasies for remaining in these mountains. They share schemes to construct elk suits and blend into the herd or hollow out our long stacks of baled hay to create hidden apartments.

In these zany plans, our residents lay bare their anxieties about going home. They fear that they will be swept back so forcefully into the fast-moving current of their work that they will lose all the gains they have made. Their worries are justified. The job of improving our society is difficult and never-ending, and there is still way too little organizational and societal support for including their own needs in the process.

At Windcall almost all our residents discover crucial pieces of their lives that they unknowingly relinquished in their zeal to make a positive difference in the world. They leave determined to reinstate activities and pleasures that provide a vital balance to the rigors of their work. Residents make plans to carve out time for hiking, painting, or writing, regular exercise and stretching, spending time with friends or sitting quietly alone. They see how, by abandoning so many of the things they enjoyed, they have neglected important parts of themselves and dismembered their own rich mix of interests and talents.

This realization leads them to look more closely at why they gave so much away in the first place and how they can guard against doing so again. They search to identify the voices demanding that they narrow their lives and risk the depletion of their bodies, minds, and spirits.

Most already know that sacrificing themselves for a just cause is not just acceptable but often expected in the social change community. At Windcall, some recognize with surprise the extent to which they have internalized this destructive notion. Perhaps for the first time, these individuals who labor so hard to empower others see how their work ethic saps their own power.

Residents also may begin to discover how difficult it is to stop putting the job first when hard work has become the primary measure of their self-worth. They have come to equate the value of what they do with the value of who they are. Many who claim an identity that is self-assured and action-oriented hardly recognize themselves early in their residency. With the sudden loss of their work, they feel insubstantial and indecisive.

When most of us experience a lapse of confidence in one area of our lives, we can reassure ourselves by remembering another in which we still feel solid. For those who focus almost exclusively on their jobs, however, the base on which they build their own sense of value has become very small. Their self-image stands solely on perseverance and achievement. If these folks try to rest, they feel their self-esteem disappear, and they must work even harder to get it back. Before they can build the inner resources to resist the pull and damage of overwork, residents must somehow break this double bind.

Cindy Marano saw clearly that her efforts for others had taken over her life: her work had crowded out a variety of pursuits that brought her satisfaction and joy. She was left feeling like a sadly diminished version of her old self. During her residency she realized that she did not have to *be* her work. Instead she could choose a way of life that left room for other interests and needs as well. But Cindy also understood that in order to succeed with that change, she would have to become a forceful advocate for herself both in the outside world and internally.

> I leave Windcall knowing that I must also fight the voices of others and those within myself that keep me from nurturing my own spirit — those voices that can lead me back to a desert of the heart.

Other residents have told us that they also have this experience of feeling emotionally barren. They arrive at Windcall dispirited from overriding their own needs and resigned to a distorted and reduced concept of themselves. Because they have habitually silenced their feelings and muted their senses, some speak of being lifeless and mechanical and of finding little left to like about who they have become. These individuals are discovering another consequence of overwork.

By becoming so narrowly focused and self-denying, they have cut themselves off from their potential for self-expansion. Their notion of who they are and what they can do has no room to grow and change. With little time for adventure or the discovery of a new passion or skill, residents get stuck. They begin to believe that a hard-working, harried, chronically tired person is the sum of who they really are.

While at Windcall, many residents realize that the most insidious and crucial damage of overwork has occurred in their relationship to themselves. Gradually they begin the process of regathering abandoned parts of their identity. Their senses awaken and they become intensely present, aware, and creative. They take risks and discover energy and optimism. Once again they feel whole, multifaceted, and full of possibility. They joke and dream and they like who they are.

As she prepared to return to her work on immigrant rights, Emily Goldfarb described the person she had found and didn't want to lose again:

What I liked best about Windcall was *myself*. I found parts of me, inner resources, places of calm and strength and serenity, a sense of self-sufficiency and equanimity that I too often lose touch with. I loved who I was at Windcall, how I chose to spend my time, how I felt in my body, in my soul.

Like Emily, what many residents desperately want to carry home and keep is a newly resilient, aware, and engaged self — and the sturdy belief in their own value that goes with it.

It took a while before Albert and I understood the depth of some of our residents' needs. We did not fully comprehend the punishment of their work. Nor did we yet understand that, like a disease, burnout whittled down the options and energies of those afflicted and weakened their ability to resist its progression.

I was able to catch my young therapists before their harmful patterns became too engrained. But all of our residents have been in the social justice field for at least five years and most show fifteen to twenty-five years on their vitae. Their habits are well established. Moreover, few have had mentors to point out and challenge the erosion taking place in their lives or to support a commitment to work that does not risk their own well-being. On the contrary, many coworkers, boards, and funders seem to do just the opposite.

We had always thought that if left unabated, burnout would finally devour an individual's energy and purpose and shut him down. Two of our residents showed us another face of its devastation. The first toiled ferociously for the rights of poor women. Her own life experience had fueled a great anger at the inequities still faced by others like herself and she was a fearless fighter on their behalf. She also taught us that while anger can be an important motivator for those pushing for social justice, if not owned and used appropriately, it can become a destructive force, as well.

At Windcall this resident was unable to leave her battlefield behind. She denigrated her fellow residents and accused them of being "soft" because they had never lived on the street. She rebelled against any limits, even the safety precautions used on trail rides. All other parts of her seemed lost to the war she now saw everywhere.

The second resident was a potent and articulate advocate for the environment. It was clear he felt every attack on our clean air and water, our forests and endangered species as if it were a personal assault. He also obviously believed all other social concerns were of less importance. He argued hard to convince the members of his group about the primacy of his issue and he trivialized their own work. Failing to win converts, he spent most of his time on the phone with those who shared his focus.

These two residents got little if anything from their time at Windcall. They arrived so well encased in their own perception of the world and their purpose in it that they could not be touched. They had totally fused with their work, and their ardor had swallowed even their human kindness. Burnout had not drained and numbed these two; a fire raged in each and had consumed everything but their passion for their own cause.

Our third important teacher was a woman who picked fruit and vegetables in the fields as a child and now labored for the rights of fellow farmworkers. She brought neither a volcano of anger nor a shield of righteousness. She carried instead a torrent of pain that she could no longer contain.

She described being a teenager on picket lines, battling for affirmative action and being jailed for civil disobedience. Then she movingly wondered aloud when she had lost hope. Had it been during the dance she attended as a young woman when an immigration raid demolished the celebration, or when she sat by the bedsides of pesticide-poisoned neighbors? Or had it happened when women from her own community rejected her pleas to help the families of other farmworkers who lost their wages when the winter harvest succumbed to an early freeze?

She had swallowed the emotional content of her life for so long that it could no longer be contained. At first she dominated all group conversations, but her fellow residents treated her with compassionate understanding and gradually her flow of words slowed enough so that she could channel them into a long, written story.

In the years after she left, we heard from her twice. Both times she credited her residency at Windcall with returning her lost spirit. She also has referred several other fine organizers to the program. Now we understand that having a safe place where all that pain could be expressed and expelled was exactly the healing she needed.

Organizers and activists for social justice are not the only people at risk for burnout. Anyone who slips or is pushed by circumstance into years dominated by debilitating work is equally vulnerable, especially if his or her task involves the needs and strife of others.

To a lesser degree, the rest of us should pay attention, too. We are no longer insulated from the pain and devastation occurring everywhere around the globe. Within minutes of any catastrophe, we are in its midst, seeing the images and hearing personally from those who are its victims. As the world seems to shrink and we realize the magnitude of its suffering, we are faced with a more urgent imperative to improve the lives of others. We, too, need to know ways of staying present and effective without compromising ourselves in the process. We must learn how to tend our relationships with each other and with ourselves in a healthy and sustaining way. We all need to protect our moments of celebrating friendship or of making tea in a red pot and quietly watching the sun rise.

Whether by honoring small, nourishing rituals or making life changes, many of our residents leave Windcall determined to incorporate what they have learned about self-healing and self-care into their lives. They write or tell us of their efforts to bring the mountain home and we discover, with great fondness and interest, how their residencies still echo through their lives.

Several have mentioned that they applied their personal insights directly to their jobs. While at Windcall, Delia Gomez found art to be the best catalyst for her own healing. When she returned to Texas, where she had worked for many years providing shelter and services to political refugees, she began a new project. She used art to address the trauma she saw in the relationships between El Paso residents and local immigrants.

Jah'Shams Abdul Mu'min came to Windcall from one of the poorest parts of Los Angeles. He left Montana with plans to bring a new ingredient to his work empowering inner-city youth. He incorporated the self-care strategies he had learned at Windcall into a new leadership-training program.

Robert Bray had spent years in the gay and lesbian rights movement but was ready to move on. He created a new organization during his time at Windcall and launched it when he returned home. The SPIN Project provides news media technical assistance to nonprofit public-interest organizations across this country that want to influence debate, shape public opinion, and attract positive coverage. Robert recalled that the idea for SPIN hit while he was furiously riding his bike back from Belgrade with a storm on his heels. He gave credit to the wide-open spaces for providing the creative dimension he needed to brainstorm and his fellow residents for helping him flesh out the idea.

Robert also wrote recently and told us how Windcall stays with him — or more accurately, how he stays with it.

> My memories are up there with the cows, the teepee, the pond, the mountains, the storms coming across the valley, and the loft of that wonderful barn where I spent many an afternoon.

Most people speak very personally about the legacy of Windcall in their lives. Betsy Barton expressed the feelings of many residents when she recently reflected on the years since she watched that iris spring open in 1997.

> My challenge since I left has been to bring Windcall into my life all the time. To take care of myself, to listen to the quiet inner voice that most of us just brush aside because we're too busy. I wish I could say I have it down pat, but unfortunately it's still a work in progress.

Several residents have written to say how they have reminders of Windcall nearby to help them resist old patterns. They use images of their Windcall experience to reinforce the possibility of new ways of feeling and being.

Three women have painted their offices what they call "Windcall green" — the calming shade of sage that is on the walls in the guesthouse and studio barn. They and many others have tacked above their desks pictures of their housemates and our holiday greeting cards, each year bearing a different image of a Windcall scene. Others simply carry Windcall inside as a place of refuge to which they can mentally and emotionally return to slow down, breathe, and get things in perspective.

Holly Finke is one of those. A year after her residency she told us how she used her experience here to deal with the rigors of work. Holly has spent years addressing a major urban justice issue across the country: the eviction of long-time low-income residents in order to upgrade a community and lure more affluent people downtown. She said she has discovered that Windcall is not just a noun or place. It is a verb that she uses when she feels stressed and off-center.

As in when work is getting to be too much, saying to myself, "OK, Holly, lets windcall that!"

She stops then and imagines herself on the guesthouse deck listening to the chirping of birds at the feeder, or in the meadow below the barn watching the changing red and magenta hues of a Montana sunset.

Sharon Streater does something similar. Sharon is the lead organizer for a network of seventeen low-to-moderate-income multiracial and interfaith congregations in Tampa, Florida. Sharon recently explained how her residency continues to affect her life.

At times I have what I call a "Windcall moment," when I close my eyes and envision the stillness and majesty of the mountains or hear the wind speaking tenderly through the leaves. Those are important moments of deep rest that still seem to help carry me through it all.

A Colombian-born immigrant raised in the state of Rhode Island and the youngest of ten children, Marielena Hincapie is now a national leader in immigration and low-wage workers' rights at the National Immigration Law Center in Los Angeles. Marielena wrote to tell us that she had scheduled regular time on her calendar for herself and had joined a nearby yoga studio.

I went back to my journal and relived what I had experienced while I was there and have begun to incorporate Windcall into my every day life in small ways. I have also made some major life decisions that are all efforts at taking care of myself and doing what is truly important to me. I firmly believe I have been able to take these steps as a result of being at Windcall and starting a healing process that is manifesting itself in my personal and professional life.

Walter Davis, the resident who wrote of being happily broadsided at a conference by a fellow resident's enthusiastic greeting, sets up a Windcall day every month where he puts all else aside and does something for fun. He also has stuck to his decision to take regular vacations. Here's what he said he had carried home from Windcall:

I learned that the personal is vital; that allowing for reflection and self-assessment at a distance from work is important. It's more than important; it has to be built in. There is too much emphasis on the immediacy of our work instead of its context.

Other residents report that they have built new structures into their lives that reflect a better understanding of their own specific needs. David Mann was the person who described the birth of his poetic self in the studio barn. He has now made room for that poet at home. A few years ago David wrote and described how much he is enjoying a writing space he and his wife put together the summer after he left Windcall.

Ellen Moore was doing extremely draining work coordinating HIV services for adolescents in San Francisco. In a letter written the year following her residency, she explained how she had grappled with her desire to move out of the inner city into a physical place that nourished her. At Windcall, Ellen wrote, she began to realize that she could be just as dedicated and committed to her work even if she did not share the living conditions of those she sought to help. Much later we ran into Ellen and she told us how she loved taking evening walks in her new, more rural neighborhood and having nearby hiking trails to wander on weekends.

Laura Gordon wanted to be an FBI agent when she was ten years old, but a letter from J. Edgar Hoover informed her that all agents were men. So she became a union organizer instead and continued that work for over twenty years in North Carolina. Four years after she left Windcall, Laura sent us an email about a major change she could now make since her grown children had just moved out.

> So I am selling my old house and I am building a small log cabin
> in the mountains. It will have an office with a Windcall computer
> counter and an exact replica of the guesthouse birdfeeder on my
> small back deck.

For Fran Barrett, who almost didn't apply because she was so embarrassed to need a break, the gift of Windcall was simply and powerfully a deep reminder of her own value.

It was really amazing to be able to walk down the road to the forest and put my feet in that little creek and just sit there for hours talking to myself. Doing that, I recognized that in this life I actually had a place. That it was okay for me to have some needs or do things that were good for me as opposed to good for everybody else. It was really a turn-around moment for me, this Windcall. That's why I say it was life changing, because up until then I really thought it was self-indulgent for me to take care of myself.

Our wish for Fran and all the residents is that they will advocate for themselves with the same determination and passion they show for others. We also hope they will understand that doing so can only strengthen their work and the chance to achieve a more just and equitable nation.

For sixteen years, we have watched this group of people we find so deserving rebuild access to their own resources of healing and renewal. We have seen them take a new sense of comfort and delight in themselves. For them Windcall has come to stand for respecting their own needs and for remembering their whole and healthy selves and whatever it is that preserves them. This is the mountain they carry home.

Here I have learned that our bodies and hearts know what they need to heal. For those of us who have been battered and wounded in our movement work, the opportunity to simply find a quiet and safe place to stop, rest, and allow ourselves to heal is invaluable. Everyone at Windcall provides not only a physical space, but more importantly, the trust in us, our work, and our ability to find what we need. All that makes the magic of Windcall possible. Trusting my body and my spirit to lead me to what I needed here was so important."

—*Taj Rashad James (2001)*

Windcall is a conversation
With myself; a dance
With my spirit; a portrait
Of my heart in balance.

We all leave ourselves here to carry on
As we have been given ourselves in return,
To carry home.

—Brenda Cummings (1999)

How do you say good-bye to Windcall?

Even though it may take a couple of days to finally believe it, there are no rules here, nothing you are supposed to do . . . you really can do whatever you feel like. Nobody tells you what your time here is to be, there are no agendas, no outline, no instructions. That's the magic of this place and this time.

But the catch is nobody tells you how to let it go. Like the rest, you have to find your own way to do that too.

I've pondered this for the last couple of days, as the time left got shorter and shorter. You can say good-bye to the people. You can even hug a horse and tell Jesse just how much you appreciated his doggish companionship—even when he's wet.

But, how do you say good-bye to the sky, ever present and ever changing, to the mountains and the stars that are always there but that you've not stopped to see for a while? How do you say good-bye to the smell of the wind or the sound of a stream or the rain? And how do you say good-bye to the freedom to act on an impulse, to sit and read as long as you want, to paint and create whatever art is in you, to walk, to sit, to think or not? To the moment when it hit you that all the profound revelations you just had, you *knew* when you were nine—that living is a lot more than being alive, that doing nothing is doing something, and that you can't really play if you think about it.

So how do you do it? How do you bring the whole thing full circle and close it? I just this morning figured it out. A couple of days after I got here, I started a painting. And about that time I also "got" Windcall—I started following my whims and stopped structuring my tasks. So I figured I would finish my painting tomorrow or the next day or whenever. Yesterday I suddenly felt pressured to get it done before I leave. After all, I had to "finish" my Windcall stuff! But this morning it hit me—I don't have to finish the painting and I don't have to finish Windcall. The circle I was trying to close is much larger than I thought.

And again, I drew from my reserve of nine-year-old facts: except for peeing, there isn't anything you gotta finish right now. Windcall is a place and Windcall is a state of mind. The sky, the stars, the wind, and the rain are at home, too, and so is the rest of it. They are all so big here you can't help but see them! Once they get your attention though, it's a lot easier to see them anywhere. So when I leave tomorrow, I'll take with me a painting I never plan to finish to remind me to step back on the circle every once in a while and find Windcall again.

—*Bill Fields (1998)*

14 Epilogue

*Windcall reminds me that if we are to humanize this work
we must find a way to humanize ourselves. We need moments
of silence and listening. We must take the time to attend to
ourselves, our own wounds and needs.*

— *The Late Rev. Dr. Mac Charles Jones (1994)*

*d*uring the sixteen years of the Windcall Resident Program, organizers
and activists taught us about the nature, difficulties, and rewards of
their work. They related the events and hopes that had propelled them into
their profession and described a work culture that demolished their energy.
They helped us understand the process of burnout, why their ranks are particularly susceptible to it, and what can reverse its toll. Most importantly, they
convinced us that the prevailing work ethic and funding practices of the social
change sector must be changed.

Our nation relies on social justice work to implement the principles of
our democracy yet does little to support such efforts. Even the non-profit community falls short of meeting the needs and goals of organizers and activists.
Too many of its institutions underestimate the importance of what inspires
and drives these men and women. Consequently they neglect practices that
would sustain their dedication and assure their longevity in the field.

Kirsten Irgens-Moller is a founder and the director of Global Exchange,
an organization that links people who work for human rights around the
world. When she explained the compelling reward that fuels her efforts, she
spoke for many.

Social justice work is a way of being that provides us with the deepest meaning of our lives.

Organizers and activists have witnessed or felt firsthand the corrosive power of injustice. From somewhere deep inside they rise up to confront it. They act from a moral imperative to empower people in our country who are denied basic rights and opportunities. In doing so, they benefit not only those whom they touch but themselves as well. Tasks that engage our deepest values also reward us deeply.

My job as a therapist fit that model for me. It also captured, challenged, and expanded me in unexpected ways. It called on more than my training. It used all of me. In the context of helping my fellow human beings, even the parts of my life that had seemed least worthwhile—fears, hurts, and failures—often were valuable guides. My work with others taught me that all of my experience was important and useful. Within me lay the multiple strands of shared humanity that link us all.

At a young age, each of us forms a sense of our own capabilities that is based primarily on how others judge us. This assessment sinks below consciousness and becomes who we think we are. As we mature we have a chance to revise that image—to redefine our self-worth and move beyond limits that in our youth we accepted as our very nature. We may look back and discover that our strengths were born from our mistakes, or see that our very capacity to care for others was forged by our own loneliness and pain. As adults, we get to gather up parts of ourselves that, earlier, we may have hidden away in shame.

Meaningful work can catalyze this process of individual healing and integration in a powerful way. Moreover, when our work and personal growth intertwine, they produce a synergy that makes our efforts sustainable. Even as we empower others, we too grow stronger and have more to bring to our jobs.

This is the healthy version of working from deep values. The social change community needs to make certain that its institutions provide the resources and supports necessary to keep this important synergy between work and personal growth alive and active. With these two in balance, the work of social change will prosper. If, however, funders and nonprofit organizations sanction self-sacrifice and victimize their own with unrealistic expectations and too little support, the flip side of working from core values will take over. When activists have only their passion to fuel their work, the endpoint is martyrdom or, in today's parlance, burnout. Both refer to a commitment that turns in on itself and devours the individual.

The residents have convinced us that if we want to strengthen those who strive for social justice we must create a new culture. It must be one that not only takes into account the reward of their work but also accurately perceives the nature of their tasks.

The social change community has assumed too many of the current values of our larger society—values that are antithetical to the very essence of social justice work. In this country we champion productivity and efficiency. Our prevailing work culture has little patience for those who engage in the painstaking task of supporting men and women as they improve individual lives and communities. Our society seems to ignore the vital importance of those of its members who teach, heal, and empower.

Nonprofit funding institutions should take into account that, unlike the for-profit sector, where speed to outcome is prized and expected, the work of social change demands that organizers invest time in building relationships of trust. That is the only way they can identify and support indigenous leaders and find solutions that truly represent and serve a diversity of communities.

Funders could shift the social change culture by changing their own practices. Currently, far too few of them are willing to provide the long-term support organizers need to build power over time. Their historical preference for single-year grants weakens projects that take longer to come to fruition. They also need to re-examine an unwritten policy of never exceeding three years of financial support to the same organization regardless of its performance. That arbitrary rule can erode an organization's effectiveness just as its work begins to yield results. Because of these two common practices, executive directors typically must spend as much as half of their time fundraising in order to keep their organizations viable. What a costly waste of their vision and leadership.

Foundations also need to recognize and address the emotional toll inherent in most social change efforts. Many organizers and activists work daily with people who are disenfranchised and despairing. They absorb a residue of distress from those efforts. Few nonprofits, however, can provide time for renewing depleted human resources. Workers have no chance to recover their emotional balance before heading, once again, into the fray.

Social change work is based on a respect for the humanity in each person. The men and women who devote their lives to it should not be excluded from that respect. When funding sources support projects, but ignore the health and well-being of the men and women responsible for their creation and operation, they are worse than shortsighted. They are potentially destructive.

Instead, they must lead the way toward creating a new, more humane work ethic. Historically, very few foundations have investigated staff working conditions, salary levels, and training and renewal opportunities as part of their evaluation of a potential grantee. In making their investment decision they have been primarily concerned with project performance. It is time they took a longer view, targeting funds and providing the oversight that will insure stronger organizations with good staff support as well as programmatic achievements. Funders must affirm the important relationship between healthy individuals, healthy organizations, and high-quality, enduring progress. Their actions would finally embed the care of leadership where it belongs—at the center of the social change agenda.

As Gary Sandusky, who works with the Center for Community Change in Idaho, put it:

> We need a culture within our organizations that rewards staff efforts
> with meaningful social change externally *and* a sense of being part of
> a group that respects and recognizes their individual growth as well.

But if the social change community is to create this new culture it must make other changes as well. Too many organizations are fearful of building into their proposals the real cost of projects; of submitting a budget that includes adequate staff care and realistic time requirements. They need to claim their own powerful role in this society and establish social change work as the legitimate and valued profession that they know it to be.

At the same time, organizations must work on another undermining force. Many of the residents admitted that they also played a role in perpetuating unhealthy expectations and practices in the nonprofit sector. They found within themselves vestiges of the outmoded and destructive work ethic that measures the value of their efforts by the price they are willing to pay. These unhealthy remnants must be acknowledged and discussed within organizations. They are responsible for limiting the quality of life of activists and organizers, their effectiveness on the job, and perhaps, for obstructing the most vital contribution they could make—modeling to others the more humane world they seek to create.

Lisa Duran directs an immigrant-based organizing project in the Denver metropolitan area—Derechos Para Todos/Rights for All People. After working for social justice for almost twenty years, she has come to understand that her own health and well-being are crucial prerequisites of effective and enduring work.

> I have found out that *who I am* — my heart, my spirit — has become
> as or more important than *what I do* for justice. I don't say that lightly,
> because our work means little if we can't achieve real and lasting
> change. But it seems to me that *how* I work comes from inside me.
> Building a more sustaining and sustainable society happens when
> we are about the business of creating loving, healthy and respectful
> relationships among and between people and institutions.

Fortunately, in trying to achieve this new culture that connects "being" with "doing," the progressive community does not have to start from scratch. Some organizations, funders, and individuals are already leading the way. These are a few.

Grassroots Leadership, a multi-racial, community-based organization in North Carolina, pays good wages and offers a dental and health insurance plan. Staff members attend scheduled retreats for training and career development. Workers receive a three-month paid sabbatical every five years. A staff phone chain keeps everyone current about one another's important life events—family tragedies, life transitions, and celebrations. Former staff members serve on the board and stay connected to current staff concerns. Si Kahn, founder and director for over twenty-five years, has dedicated himself to creating and maintaining this healthy and equally productive work environment.

One of the first entities to build reflective time into leadership development was the Alston/Bannerman Fellowship Program in Baltimore, Maryland. For over eighteen years it has offered longtime activists of color three-month paid sabbaticals during which they can pursue educational or renewal opportunities.

The Durfee Foundation focuses its support on nonprofit leaders in its own Los Angeles area. It offers stipends and expenses to six individuals each year for renewal in any manner they propose.

Wilburforce Foundation in Seattle, Washington, has dedicated itself to preserving the remaining wild places in this country. Its directors obviously understand the relationship between their goal and the well-being of the individuals working to achieve it. Every one of its environmental grants includes money for organizational capacity building and leadership training assistance.

One foundation has diminished the geographical isolation of many small organizations and helped them to teach each other. With its Grassroots Exchange Fund, Northern California's Common Counsel Foundation promotes interaction between social justice nonprofits throughout the United States. The fund offers quickly available travel grants to small nonprofits that want to participate in collaborative campaigns or access technical assistance.

In an effort close to our own hearts, former residents are working to continue the Windcall model. The mission of their new organization, the Windcall Institute, is to sustain and develop social justice leadership by offering leaders opportunities for spiritual, psychological, and physical renewal. In addition they will provide continuing education on renewal practices and on the art of sustaining leaders in the social justice sector.

With more models like these, we will shape a progressive culture that promotes the essential connection between efforts to empower others and nurture our own shared human values and social action. We will create the community of common purpose needed to make enduring social change.

August, 2005
Summer is short in Montana. Even in the lingering heat of August we find harbingers of the coming fall. The serviceberry and chokecherry bushes are bent low with purple fruit. The rose hips and sticky geranium leaves flash

orange and red-gold in the undergrowth. Tall stalks of lupine seedpods line the driveway and today I saw the first thistles scattering their seeds to the wind.

Ted has finished stacking and covering the huge golden rounds of hay and the combines drone across the valley as they thresh our neighbors' grain. On our early walks we hear the elk moving in the woods and catch a vagrant waft of cool, clear air left by the night.

The waning summer is not the only ending I feel. For the first August in thirteen years, Jesse no longer sits expectantly on the doorstep ready to burst into puppy-like leaps when we join him for our daybreak explorations. We scattered his ashes and many tears on this land that he knew and loved completely.

In a few days, the last season of residents will begin their Windcall adventure. I almost can't imagine the years ahead without these twice-monthly arrivals of our remarkable guests. During the last sixteen years, they have been the best of company, never failing to move us with their courage and commitment. They, like Jesse, have not only left their tracks on this land but on our hearts as well.

Running the Windcall Resident Program has been a joyous experience for both Albert and me. It truly has been a work of our hearts, and as such, it has given back in equal measure everything that we brought to it. As we close this segment of our lives, we will carry with us memories of more than 400 shared adventures that led residents through bone-jarring first horse trots, long mountain hikes, laughter-filled dinner conversations, and quiet rediscoveries of self. We feel honored to have been part of their journeys.

In a world where the forces of darkness hold sway far too often, it is important to create models of an alternative value set, just as Windcall does. This is a place, both physical and spiritual, that I will hold dear during the battles that surely lie ahead.

—*Mary Lassen (2005)*

Seven Profiles
by Sally Lehrman

Scott Douglas

"I try to be as revolutionary as justice
and as subversive as love."

It was 1982, and Reverend Mike Harper was presenting Scott Douglas to the board of the Greater Birmingham Ministries (GBM), an interfaith social justice organization in the Deep South. Forty-seven Alabama church people, mostly white, sat assembled around the wooden tables. "I'd like to recommend Scott Douglas," Harper told the assembled group. "He's a subversive and a revolutionary."

Harper clearly meant the introduction as a compliment, but for Douglas the words registered with a shock. He really wanted a.seat on the board — and these religious leaders might disapprove of a black radical in their midst. Thinking quickly, he explained to the group, "I try to be as revolutionary as justice and as subversive as love."

"Whew!" Douglas remembers, laughing. The board members' faces relaxed. Eleven years later Douglas became the Ministries' first African American executive director, in charge of the whole operation. And while he hardly fits the stereotype of an underground radical, there was some truth to Harper's assessment. In fact, Douglas *was* a member of the Communist Party and had developed his social justice know-how as a district organizer in Birmingham, working on economic justice, equal rights, and peace issues. He admired and learned from both Gus Hall, the Party's general secretary, and chairman Henry Winston, a legendary strategist, movement builder, and social analyst.

In the Party Douglas perfected his ability to build bridges between people of differing cultures and belief systems, a talent essential to his work with the Ministries. Participants are black and white, Christian and Jew, and one day, Douglas hopes, more will be Muslim as well. "We are people of faith who struggle for justice in community," Douglas explains. The task is not easy. Working consciously across religious and racial differences is unusual anywhere in the country, especially in the South. There, the divisions are deep — even within a given denomination — and the religious right is pressing hard for a very different sort of dream.

The Communist Party helped Douglas see the separation between people in the South as not only the inheritance of slavery but also the tool long kept sharp by wealthy landowners and corporations in order to divide workers and maximize profits. U.S. Steel, for instance, tolerated Ku Klux Klan rallies behind its gates. "A lot of folks don't even know it, but we're living with the residue of that history," Douglas explains. "Black people and white people in the South are the most intimate strangers. We know so much and hide so much about our relationships together. The legacy of slavery has been this duality of memory, duality of history, duality of reality."

Now Douglas must cross racial and religious lines on a regular basis. He does so with warmth and humor, developing relationships and challenging assumptions with a quiet effectiveness. One recent Sunday he spent the morning worshipping with the Saint Paul United Methodist Church congregation at their special Twenty-First Harvest Celebration. He gave a member of the choir a ride home, then headed up to a wealthy area of Birmingham to join a five-kilometer walk to raise money for hunger- and poverty-fighting programs, including his own. The day before, he had attended a conference for the progressive New South Coalition in nearby Huntsville, where participants discussed strategies for achieving voter rights for former prison inmates and responding to attacks against black and other progressive leaders.

Dressed smartly that Saturday in a tan checked sport coat and slacks,

"We, as a faith-based organization, must always be in constant conversation with the poor. Their stories are rivers flowing by us and as we listen and listen, out of those stories flows our agenda."

Douglas had lugged around a faded orange cloth cooler full of brochures declaring the need for a new Alabama constitution shaped by citizen delegates. "It would be the first constitutional convention of people who look like Alabama in the state's history," Douglas reminded the assembly. Among other things, proposed changes would undo taxes that unequally burden the poor, and free up monies for sorely needed public infrastructure. The campaign is central to Greater Birmingham Ministries' organizing arm, which targets the inequities built into social institutions such as housing and transportation.

Douglas's first encounter with GBM had been in 1976 as a client, a newcomer to the city, out of a job and looking for free clothes for his two-year-old son, Fred. Today he has been at the helm for just over a decade, having helped the thirty-eight-year-old interfaith, interracial ministry grow from a budget of about $300,000 to $1.2 million a year. Sixty-two board members meet weekly or monthly in working groups to decide on priorities within each of its mission areas.

Fundamentally, the two-story structure a few blocks from the convention center is a "social change incubator," Douglas says. The modest building could be any office, except for the eight-foot Peace Pole out front with its messages of peace in six languages. Most of the first floor is dedicated to direct service. On a normal morning, at least three dozen people line up along the block for clothing, food, or financial assistance with rent, utility bills, or medical payments. Last year GBM served about 7,600 residents through foundation grants and contributions from its eighteen member churches and synagogues. This work goes deeper than the desire to help less fortunate people. "We, as a faith-based organization, must always be in constant conversation with the poor," Douglas says. "Their stories are rivers flowing by us and as we listen and listen, out of those stories flows our agenda."

Upstairs, staff and member organizations develop campaigns to change the systems that push people into dire need in the first place. Architectural drawings lean against one wall of the conference room. The sketches may help protect an historic black neighborhood from being swallowed up by a rich Birmingham suburb and replaced with condominiums and offices. Another effort presses for better public transportation so that people without cars can get to work dependably and on time.

"Part of our work is to increase the infrastructure of social change — social betterment, economic betterment — in the city," Douglas explains. GBM has spun off sixteen independent direct-service and organizing entities so far. But Douglas also is talking about the human infrastructure. Bringing religious communities together to work on justice issues is a challenge in itself, let alone forging a faith agenda that unites them all. At the moment, GBM includes Jews, Catholics, Methodists, Unitarians, and one Muslim from both low- and high-income congregations. Conversations with the Birmingham Islamic Society are under way, and next Douglas hopes to reach out to the African-American Pentecostal Church of God in Christ. Eventually participants hope to create an Alabama Faith Council that can respond loudly and clearly to activist Christian conservatives, countering what Douglas calls "right-wing denial faith" with a message of faith-based social justice. "We consider ourselves like the church mouse, we just run around and do our stuff, but next year we've got to become bolder," Douglas says. "Our job is to be the Jeremiahs and Ezekiels, to become the prophetic voices who speak truth to power."

People from different regions, races, genders, sexual orientations, or of different immigrant status need to avoid the "one-downsmanship" game, which only gives more power to the privileged few, Douglas says. "All of the oppressed become part of a competitive mix and struggle over meager civil, economic, and social crumbs," he explains, "rather than rising together to claim the cake of human rights for all and even speak to the stewardship of all creation — all Earth."

Scott Douglas hadn't intended to become a revolutionary. As a child he loved aircraft and the sciences, especially engineering and physics, because they could teach him how to build things that could fly. In the sixth grade he and his friends decided to test their talents. Angry at the abrupt dismissal of a young, pretty substitute teacher, the boys attempted to get back at the principal. They built a rocket and aimed it at their school. "Based on my chemical calculations I think it would have worked, but it went 'splat' instead of 'boom,'" Douglas recalls, acknowledging that the collaborators could have caused serious damage. The children covered their tracks (and the big black hole in the ground) with a story involving hot dogs and knocking over the grill. One grew up to become a NASA engineer.

Social justice was far from the young Douglas's mind, despite the burgeoning civil rights movement and historic lunch-counter sit-ins there in Nashville in 1960. He read lots of books about flying and, since those usually involved the military, he leaned toward the political right. In 1963, he recalls, he became the first black teen in Nashville, Tennessee, to win a city essay contest with a treatise arguing for U.S. world domination and its right to fly over other countries' territories. When he accepted the award, Douglas didn't even notice that he had to sit in a separate section from the white students and their families. And when Mrs. Burgess, his high school English teacher, took him to see *To Kill a Mockingbird*, she had to call the students' attention to the fact that they sat in the balcony, just like the black citizens of Maycomb who watched Tom Robinson unfairly convicted of raping a white girl. "It was normal," Douglas explains.

Douglas was drawn to a five-year program at the University of Tennessee that combined engineering and physics with liberal arts. "The premise was that engineers couldn't think and scientists couldn't build anything — the idea was to build a bridge," Douglas says. "That really appealed to me." He was thrilled to get a student loan. But one day he learned that a white friend he was tutoring in physics was at school on a full scholarship, even though he had far lower test scores. The race-based inequities built into America crystallized for Douglas, and he sank into a depression that deepened when Reverend Martin Luther King, Jr., was murdered. After finishing school Douglas got work at an aircraft factory, but he hated the racism he encountered in the union. By then he had joined the Communist Party and often would distribute the *Daily Worker* around the plant. When the defense plant won its next big contract, he wasn't called back.

Douglas had married his college sweetheart, Lynn, and when she got a scholarship to the University of Alabama's master's program in early childhood education, they decided to go. Douglas went from one job to another in Birmingham until he landed some work with the Southern Organizing Committee for Economic and Social Justice. Organizing turned out to be a good fit and soon he joined the Communist Party staff. His job included selling the *Daily Worker* to employees driving through the gates into the U.S. Steel plant. While many would buy it, others tried to break his outstretched arm by pinning it against their moving truck. Later he did a stint as a Sierra Club organizer on environmental justice, developing alliances between blacks, poor whites, and wealthy members.

When the opening for executive director at Greater Birmingham Ministries came up, Douglas had been a volunteer there for eleven years. "I said, how great to be paid for that," he recalls. In the Communist Party, he had been a member of the religious caucus. For him and other religious members, socialism was a means of serving their faith. "To recognize the connections between justice, compassion, and humility and to be able to sustain yourself working on that is very important to me," he says.

It's not that Douglas had always been attracted to the church. Even though his mother would take him to revivals, he never stepped forward. "I said, 'Ma, ain't nobody call me.'" It took free dinners Tuesdays and Thursdays to get him to become the first black member of Epworth Methodist Church in Knoxville, Tennessee, when he was in college. What Douglas calls "comic-book" faith, the faith of people who are not challenged by God, scared him. Church leaders even forced him off a Methodist committee because of his Communist affiliations. But at the same time, he decided not to let the church push him away. As a child he had searched for meaning in life and read the Bible on his own. His family discussed the lessons in the sermon and he liked Sunday School, where he learned about the struggle of the Hebrews and its parallels with the history of oppression of black people in the United States.

Now, as executive director of an interfaith ministry, Douglas may be finally answering the call his mother had hoped he would hear. Living his faith really does require becoming a revolutionary, he believes — and struggling for a radical vision of justice, compassion, and human community. He quotes Micah 6:8 to explain: ". . . and what does the Lord require of you but to do justice, and to love kindness, and to walk humbly with your God." He adds, "That's me. That's what I aspire to."

Pamela Chiang

"We need to be tangible and specific,
and you know what? We can win."

Pamela Chiang and a Laotian elder, Thongsoun Phuthama, had just finished giving a talk about their fight for a new, multilingual toxic alert to students at the University of California at Berkeley. As they walked down the concrete steps of Wheeler Hall together, the former janitor turned to Chiang. "I can't believe I have given class instruction in a place where I have mopped floors," he said in Lao, with a bilingual friend translating. Now, a decade later, Phuthama's words, powerful and sweet, stay with Chiang. While it was a casual remark, it summarized all that Chiang believes in as an organizer.

Chiang sees her work as a means to hand people back their own power and identity, to restore their dignity. "You as elders, you as teenagers, you have a voice," she remembers telling Phuthama and the other Lao, Mien, Khmu, and Hmong refugees she worked with in Richmond, California. Forced to leave agrarian, preliterate societies in Laos, they had arrived in the San Francisco Bay Area only to contend day after day with low-paying jobs, dangerous working conditions, and deadly refinery blasts in their backyards. But over time, with some pushing, practicing, and a lot of courage, they found their strength to demand something better.

Like Thongsoun, Chiang's mother, grandparents, and older brother also immigrated to San Francisco. But they came from Taiwan, where the family had migrated in the 1940s to escape the Japanese invasion of mainland China. They settled in the Clement Street Chinatown area and her mother made a living selling Asian art. Today Chiang applies lessons gleaned from that time in order to bridge many distances of history, geography, and experience. In Texas she stood shoulder-to-shoulder with Latina garment workers who were fired abruptly when Levi's shut down its jeans manufacturing plant. In California she relied on simultaneous translation in three languages to help the Laotian immigrants formulate their demands. In South Dakota she pulled out a clipboard and interviewed dozens of Lakota Nation basketball fans, hoping to spur interest in community organizing. Standing about five-foot-three, with fine long hair, a simple clarity of purpose and humility of spirit guide her. "I was pushed by mentors — you just do it. You do it in a way that respects the culture, whatever it is," Chiang says.

Chiang concentrates on leadership training and coaching as a field organizer with the Center for Community Change (CCC). Among other projects, she has been charged with developing a grassroots effort to address the deep-rooted problem of hunger in the rural Great Plains states. In a 2003 survey of 403 poor households, CCC found that nearly one in five families sometimes did not have enough to eat. Three-quarters of American Indian families living on reservations said they sometimes run out of food and have no money to buy more. More than one-quarter of parents felt their children didn't get the nutrients they needed. CCC decided to use the issue as an opening to build power for Native Americans and to link their concerns with those of low-income, rural whites.

Chiang commuted to South Dakota for months in order to develop the relationships and infrastructure necessary to get the anti-hunger push off the ground. One recent fall, with the help of an intern, she opened an office in a little church in Rapid City. Soon thereafter she was attending basketball games at the four-day Lakota Nation Invitational Tournament with a small group of American Indian leaders from the church, the high school and Indian Health Services. The gathering attracts more than 7,500 youth and adults from hundreds of miles away, bringing together athletes, scholars, and tribal officials. They partake in a wide range of activities: sports, of course, and

*"Environmental justice was a way to put
our intellects and hearts together."*

also a science fair, a language bowl, a juried art show, and meetings on issues such as health, environment, law enforcement, and treaty concerns. "There were big names there, all the way to little kids," Chiang says. It was perfect for organizing.

Her group spread out with ten-minute surveys and managed to collect 175 attendees' views. More than half of the people they met wanted to get involved. Even though the Native American organizing effort mostly has gone well, Chiang finds she must build trust among people who repeatedly have been burned by outsiders. She remembers visiting one local activist leader who attacked her legitimacy and told her that by involving people without regard to their tribal standing, she was out of line. "She was jacking me up. I'm listening and learning—you just have to take it all in," Chiang says, describing how she respectfully heard the woman out. Warm and funny one moment, Chiang can easily switch on a commanding, no-nonsense demeanor the next. When working across cultures, she says, "You have to be ready, learning, talking with people — just being yourself." Then she added, "In the end, you just have to deliver."

Sometimes the pressure has been overwhelming as Chiang struggled to keep up with her responsibilities. If she's not traveling, she's in Montana prepping for her next out-of-town tour. "I never can feel quite ahead enough," she laments. She was especially torn by a desire to jump into the work in South Dakota with both feet, to move there temporarily in order to show her commitment and speed up the plan to inspire local leaders. But there's another pull—a family and place that have become her anchor. Chiang moved to Windcall five years ago when she and ranch manager Ted Bryan decided to join their lives. A pageant-like marriage marked the moment, complete with a brilliant red Chinese gown for the black-haired bride and a horse-drawn hay wagon to carry the beaming newlyweds. One week before their four-year anniversary, Alessandro Bo San Bryan was born. With his name, his parents designated the young boy "protector of the mountains."

In their Bar None ranching business, Chiang has joined Bryan in raising purebred Corriente cattle to sell and lease for team roping or steer wrestling, or as breeding stock. She has learned to ride a horse, mend fences, help Ted separate the calves from the cows, move the cattle from one pasture to another, and vaccinate them. "It's the one place in my life where when you get a job done, it's done, you know?" she points out. Instead of pushing for change that happens slowly and unevenly, "You have to get into the mind of a cow. Wow." When people come to help brand in the summer, Chiang cooks up feasts that blend Chinese, Italian, and Western influences in dishes like star anise stew with elk meat. She looks out her window and can check on Xiao Hong, an orphan calf that turned into a pet. "It means Little Red," Chiang says fondly with a laugh. "Except by now, she's really big."

Other than the cooking and entertaining, life on the ranch is all new for her. But out here, amid the ever-present cycle of life and death, the drama of each season, and a house on the side of a mountain, she feels herself turning inward. "The place is almost an incubator for who I am," she says. In the interdependent ranching world of Montana, the outspoken activist inside her must change strategies. It's a challenge to create new relationships and to sustain the old ones across many miles. She's a ranch woman, an urban and rural organizer, a mother, an immigrant's daughter. And much of the time, she says, she feels alone.

Chiang grew up speaking Cantonese and Mandarin in a San Francisco neighborhood populated mostly by Chinese families, then moved twelve miles north to the small town of Mill Valley. In fourth grade all of a sudden she was one of only two Chinese-American children in school. Her family lived in the flatlands, not in the wealthier hills. The other kids called her names and she vividly remembers telling one boy he was a "discriminator." That summer when her mother suggested she try swimming at the nearby recreation center, she obeyed. Before she knew it, she was excelling at the sport. Instead of "that Chinese girl," she became the swimmer. The neighborhood children might still taunt her, she remembers, "But if you kick their butts in the pool, that changes things." Swimming became a refuge of motion and rhythm, a place where she could discover her own capabilities and her ability to master something.

Chiang wanted to grow up to be a doctor who could blend traditional Chinese and Western medicine in her practice. Once she graduated from high school and arrived at UC Berkeley, though, she found herself drawn elsewhere. As she passed by the tables set up near Sather Gate, she learned about environmental issues and even joined the movement to save the ancient redwood forests. But the mainstream environmental organizations didn't seem to have room for people of color. In fact, activists seemed to consider ethnic minorities part of the problem. When Chiang discovered the environmental justice movement, she finally felt she had found her place. She and like-minded students created a campus organization, "Nindakin," which they named after a Dakota word expressing "I am the Earth." They developed their own fifteen-week course that brought community activists into classes and sent students out on internships. The group connected with Chinatown garment workers who had vision problems from all the close work and met African-Americans who could barely breathe the air in their neighborhoods. They helped fight off a toxic waste incinerator in Kettleman City, California, and visited farmworkers who couldn't avoid exposure to pesticides nearly every day. "Our education was huge," Chiang remembers. "Some of us barely graduated."

The students raised money to go to the October 1991 People of Color Environmental Justice Summit in Washington, D.C., and were thrilled to join 650 attendees in all. But Chiang and her friends noticed only a smattering of Asian Americans in the crowd. That's when they decided to form the Asian Pacific Environmental Network (APEN). They were disappointed to discover that there weren't many groups to link in a "network," though, so they looked for places to begin grassroots organizing themselves. Their research led them back to Richmond, where contamination plagued the air, water, and land. While African Americans and Latinos all lived, fished, and grew their vegetables there amidst the toxins, a growing settlement of Laotians had the least power and access to information and services. The graduates became organizers in earnest.

They began teaching residents about lead in ceramics and mercury in the fish that swim in the bay. They started a neighborhood garden and hit on the idea of working with Laotian girls. The teens were a cultural bridge between traditional families and a new society. The project would be a way to bring together young women from different Laotian ethnic groups to talk about their shared histories and to explore new problems like sex, drugs, neighborhood violence, and low self-esteem. The goal was to create a new generation of female leaders. "It was a long, long investment," Chiang remembers.

Then, in March 1999, an explosion at the Chevron Richmond refinery spewed bright orange flames for hours, belching a huge mushroom of black smoke. "We realized, holy hell, we'd better do something," Chiang says. The "shelter-in-place" emergency warnings didn't go out right away and more than twelve hundred people ended up in emergency rooms because of breathing problems and irritated eyes. It was the second refinery accident in just over a month, and it spurred APEN to shift gears.

The automated phone alerts not only had gone out late, but they were exclusively in English. Most families had no idea what had happened until they already had been exposed. Then, as APEN attempted to bring residents together to talk about the accident, the organizers realized they faced the same set of language problems. At first the team translated into three languages, but still some people were left out. "We had to go out and get ideas, research them, then translate them in a way that was accessible and meaningful. We quickly shifted into graphics mode," Chiang says. Using clip art they found in software programs, the team created symbols for ideas that might come up. They laid them all out on butcher paper so everyone could follow the meeting, have a say, and give feedback. Chiang tried to figure out when to step back and when to push the group forward. She was learning and coaching at the same time, hoping to help participants grow, and desperately wanting them to succeed.

Finally they were ready with their demand: a multilingual emergency phone alert system. The head of the Health Services Department hemmed and hawed, so they decided to move on to the county supervisors. As the Laotian delegation climbed the red steps of the Martinez courthouse to meet with their elected officials, Chiang could see the fear in their posture and hear it in their footsteps. But they had learned that they must look these powerful people in the eyes and remember how deeply the county's neglect had hurt their families. They had turned themselves from Mien, Laotian, and Khmu immigrants, from insecure teens, dutiful workers, and family garden caretakers, into leaders. They did win a commitment from the county and the new system finally went into effect in 2005. "Up until then, I was always a soldier who had to do what I was told," one man told Chiang. "You've given me a way to give back to my own community."

Bob Fulkerson

"We don't give them enough credit for their
broadmindedness, their openmindedness.
People fear what they don't know."

The women from the Reno-Sparks Indian Colony love to tease "Bobaloo" about the lap-dance incident. As they settle into a board meeting of the Progressive Leadership Alliance of Nevada (PLAN), they allude to it, their voices full of suggestion. "We'll have to explain later," tribal council member Michon Eben says with a sly laugh.

They move on to business. Michon and two other colony members have come to explain why the tribe wants to take over public lands in the Hungry Valley just north of Reno. Propping up a map of the region on a folding chair, they tell the people around the table that the colony already plans to buy mineral rights to six thousand valley acres. Members hope to extend their reach all the way up to the ridgelines. While the move by the federal government to privatize lands around Reno might seem an environmentalist's nightmare, Eben makes the case that in this situation, it's actually just the opposite. The prospering tribe wants oversight, not development rights. "We want to make sure future generations have this pristine valley," she says. "We want to make sure it's managed, protected—not only for ourselves but for you guys as well."

PLAN brings together forty groups with sometimes disparate goals, which include controlling growth, protecting water, supporting the building trades, and advocating for immigrants. But at root, they all share a vision of racial, economic, and environmental justice. The Sierra Club and the Conservation League, with their campaigns against groundwater exports to new urban areas, may seem at odds with the building trades, who make their living from new construction. The Indian Colony, with its plan to bring in Wal-Mart for economic development, may frustrate the AFL-CIO and the Nevada Interfaith Council, who listed the corporate giant in their Book of Shame for violating labor laws. Somehow, however, Bob Fulkerson, PLAN's state director, manages to help them all find common ground. His most effective tools may be a warm greeting, a wink when things get trying, and a grin that lets everyone in. "It's through relationships you bring people together," Fulkerson says. "You make people realize it's about the person next to them."

Tall and lanky, his feet planted in Ugg sheepskin boots, Fulkerson looks like the fifth-generation Nevadan he is. When Fulkerson stops in for a quick dinner at the local Taco del Mar, nearly everyone who comes in seems to know him. He can schmooze as easily with the son of casino magnate John Ascuaga as he can with a newspaper subscription salesperson active in the NAACP. He keeps his fishing gear handy in his office, the front room of a Victorian house in Reno. Sitting at his desk, he can watch the rushing Truckee River in front of him, a wall of snapshots of family, friends, and PLAN events at his back. A ruffled white apron hangs high on the wall near the door. "That's Grandma's," he explains. She painted an oak on it and detailed all the branches of the Fulkerson family tree. On his mother's side, his great-great-grandmother sailed around Cape Horn on her father's ship to San Francisco, where she met a handsome Irishman visiting from Wadsworth, Nevada. They soon married, and one hundred and fifty years ago spent their honeymoon in Lake House, across the river from Fulkerson's present-day office. Another great-great-grandfather, John, partnered with his sister, Mary, to become wagon-train masters of the first wagons along the Oregon Trail.

Fulkerson insists that lots of progressives live in Nevada. But activism in this right-to-work, conservative state isn't easy. Before PLAN helped them get started, there were no Latino, gay and lesbian, low-income, or youth advocacy

"What Bob taught me that day was something very powerful:
how to organize, how to take a stand."

organizations. On hot-button issues like immigration, a protest can deepen divisions rather than help move things forward: Yet over time, PLAN has managed to tap into the social conscience that many Nevadans seem to share but find little opportunity to express. Its members have pushed through groundbreaking worker health and safety laws, gay and lesbian nondiscrimination protections, hate-crime provisions, and comprehensive conservation safeguards despite more than two decades of a Republican-controlled state Senate. "Whenever they do something right, you drop a note in the mail," Fulkerson says. "People have long memories here. This is a small state."

Friends say Fulkerson has built up credibility across many interest groups by staying on top of every issue important to residents and creatively pushing for change. "He has a conscience that presents a clear vision and he doesn't back down," says John Drakulich, an insurance agent and long-time PLAN donor. Like Fulkerson, Drakulich is openly gay. He always takes his partner, Andy, to company events. In a state like Nevada, that means "you feel different and you always work harder," Drakulich says. Pain washes over his face as he recalls the 1994 murder of a friend, William Douglas Metz, stabbed twenty-two times by a skinhead who wanted to kill a gay man.

Drakulich and Fulkerson, whose brothers were friends, met at a birthday party for Fulkerson's partner at the time. Fulkerson still remembers how he chewed out Drakulich for marching in the Gay Pride Parade in New York but doing nothing in his hometown. "You've got to build community where you are," he insisted. In 1999 they worked together to start A Rainbow Place, a gay and lesbian community center for northern Nevada.

Fulkerson had left Nevada at eighteen to major in international relations at George Washington University. While in the capital in the late 1970s, he interned for Senator Paul Laxalt, a Republican from Nevada who was a close friend of Ronald Reagan's. "I wanted political experience and needed money," Fulkerson explains. "I wanted to become governor." The job was a blast. It opened powerful doors. But as Fulkerson walked home from Reagan's 1981 inaugural ball at the Air and Space Museum, the chilly night presented him with contradictions he couldn't stomach. He felt like he had stepped out of the court of Louis XIV into a stark hell, with steam appearing to rise right through the bodies of homeless people tucked into doorways. Fulkerson decided to go home to the desert.

Fulkerson finished school at the University of Nevada, Reno, where he read Stephen Crane, Herman Melville, and Mark Twain. He worked in a church basement at a tutoring clinic for children of the Reno-Sparks Indian Colony. He began volunteering for Citizen Alert, a group that, while he was in Washington, had successfully fought off plans to place MX missiles in tunnels throughout Nevada and move them around underground in order to avoid Soviet surveillance. Ranchers, miners, and environmentalists had united to protect the desert. By 1982, the state had once again become a target—this time as the number one choice for nuclear waste storage. Citizen Alert swung into action.

Fulkerson left for Iowa in 1984 to work on Alan Cranston's "peace and jobs" presidential campaign. As the liberal California senator's national prospects sank, Fulkerson got a call from Citizen Alert about a job. He showed up in cutoffs for the interview, but no one seemed to mind. He was hired as state director and soon was traveling all over Nevada, visiting ranchers, miners, and American Indians, bringing suburbanite environmentalists along as he stopped by homes deep in the sagebrush along dirt roads. Although Fulkerson says he learned leadership in the Boy Scouts, the time he spent in Washington had made him a very effective organizer, too. He had watched people in power, seen them work, observed as they cut deals and brokered their influence. Together the Nevadans quashed underground nuclear testing, united against the Yucca Mountain nuclear waste dump, and fought off Las Vegas' attempts to pipe groundwater from eastern and southern Nevada to new suburbs.

After a decade with Citizen Alert, Fulkerson decided to start PLAN, a coalition that would bring together Nevada's progressive social, economic, and environmental organizations. He invited unions, social service groups,

"You don't want your tactics to get stale. It makes organizing more fun, and it keeps your opponent surprised."

the NAACP, and Nevada Urban Indians to join. One by one, the coalition seeded new progressive efforts by providing office space, staffing, training, and other support until an organization could spin off on its own. When an anti-immigrant "White People's Party" filed with the secretary of state, for instance, PLAN decided to respond. After a series of community forums and a state demographic analysis, the Nevada Immigrant Coalition, staffed and run by PLAN, was formed in January 2006.

If PLAN is an incubator for progressive organizations, Bob Fulkerson is the mother hen. He puts on a fresh pot of coffee for a board meeting and walks around the table with the pot, cups, and cream. "Oh that's great, that's great," he encourages the loquacious union leader. He can barely sit still during a regional growth task force meeting, but he scribbles notes in his composition book and lets others take the lead. When he needs a rancher's attention, he pays the family a visit. If there's no phone, he sends a fax to the nearest community center and asks someone to drive it out. Little by little, he is leading Nevada's rural residents from concerns about water into relationships that bring them closer to immigrant issues, gay rights, and other PLAN priorities. "We don't give them enough credit for their broad-mindedness, their open-mindedness," Fulkerson says. Whether reviewing posters for a rally or plotting strategy, his delight in social justice work really is infectious.

The three tribes that make up the Reno-Sparks Indian Colony and its 847 members have been a part of PLAN since the beginning. In 1986 they had expanded from their 28-acre colony in Reno to a 1,950-acre reservation ten miles north in Hungry Valley. A prospering tribe, they ran five smoke shops, a nursery, a Taco Bell, and a Mercedes-Benz dealership. With the move out of the city, the tribe launched Shoshone and Washoe language classes, created a traditional hand drum group, and revived pine nut picking and other traditional practices. But they were caught by surprise when Chicago-based

Oil-Dri Corporation leased the mineral rights for 5,900 acres bordering the colony, where the cat litter maker planned to build a series of open pit clay mines and a processing plant.

Eben and her friend Darlene Gardipe, who both are now on the PLAN board, tell how PLAN and its coalition members girded them to take on Oil-Dri. "Bob taught us how to do mail-outs, a media campaign, posters," Eben says. Gardipe continues, "He was giving us a lot of help, encouragement, support, and advice. The tribe really had never had to deal with anything like that before."

Fulkerson suggested that several colony members and a few from PLAN buy seven-dollar shares of Oil-Dri stock so they could voice their concerns at the company stockholders' meeting. They arrived two days early and set up shop at the American Indian Center of Chicago. They made posters, called on local native chapters, and organized a drum group.

On the day of the meeting they set their literature out with the company materials and distributed themselves around the room. They were so upset they could hardly eat or drink at the time, but now they tell the story with glee. "They talked about the proposed plantation in Ne-vah-dah," Eben mimics the executives. She remembers with disgust how they told shareholders that the "ignorant" Indians had cost them $1 million so far. Then, she recalls, one disheveled stockholder asked the chief executive, "Do you like cats?"

"I hate cats," he answered.

But when the CEO promised to have the Nevada plant up and running by the following September, Gardipe's sister, Diane, stood up and told the chief executive that he would do no such thing.

It turns out the "lap dance" refers to a tense moment when Diane stood up again and demanded, as a member of a sovereign nation, to be heard. After she had spoken, her knees buckled and she tumbled into Fulkerson's lap. It wasn't funny at the time. The members of the colony were furious and some were close to tears. But the incident has come to symbolize the challenge taken on by "this little tribe in Nevada, standing up to a multimillion-dollar company," Gardipe marvels.

As the shareholders poured out onto the street, a drum group was already playing. Fulkerson quickly organized the protest group on street corners for maximum visual impact, and people began to march and chant. Soon lunchtime passersby were picking up signs and joining them, Eben recalls. "We started with six people. The next thing there were sixty," she says. "Then the board of directors came out and we're there still.

"What Bob taught me in that day was something very powerful: how to organize, how to take a stand."

When the group got back to Reno, everyone in town was talking about them. And finally, Oil-Dri pulled out. "I think they realized they needed a new strategy because they weren't dealing with dumb Indians," Eben says. Since then, the colony has become more involved with the NAACP and its Hispanic neighbors. Gardipe joined the racial justice committee, working both within and outside PLAN to tackle racism. Members participated in a recent peace walk and donated a billboard to promote voting rights for former felons.

Gardipe and Eben now get a nine-cent stock dividend from Oil-Dri every six months for their trouble. "PLAN showed us the activist way," Eben says. "That you have rights. That you have a vote. It gave our people pride back."

Leah Wise

"You cannot spend the majority of your hours in an
oppressive, unhealthy workplace, and go out and be
a participant in democracy."

Organizer Leah Wise knows that change in the South will require more than
a campaign for workplace safety here, a push for job protections there. For
generations, segregation and a largely race-based class system have fed worker
exploitation and hindered social progress. Now, at the same time Mexican
immigrants settle into towns and fill the lowest tier of jobs, the black people
who traditionally have populated factories are feeling the ground eroding
beneath their feet. They watch punitive social policies harden, hard-won
labor protections vanish, and their own opportunities dwindle. A new layer of
black-Latino tension has arisen, undermining efforts to organize against historical white supremacy and the corporate practices that hurt everyone.

In the early 1990s, after a decade of consolidation and job losses, both
immigrants and native-born people flocked to the South for work. They
found jobs on farms and in food processing, along with manufacturing, construction and services. The number of foreign-born residents exploded,
increasing by almost 400 percent during the decade to about 379,000 in
North Carolina alone. Between 1990 and 2000, this rural state led all others
in attracting native and foreign-born Latinos. White migrants and African-
Americans came too. Beneath the veneer of opportunity, though, poverty and
exploitation festered.

At Imperial Foods in Hamlet, North Carolina, men and women toiled for a little over minimum wage—about six dollars an hour—cutting, breading, frying and freezing chicken pieces for restaurants. In a tragic incident there in 1991, twenty-five people died and more than fifty others were injured when a hydraulic line broke, exploding into a fireball that spewed toxic smoke. The workers tried to escape, but found the exit doors locked.

During that era, companies relished the cheap labor and lax regulations they found in the South. But when globalization and free trade policies brought them even better prospects elsewhere, executives started to pull their factories out. Plants closed and jobs disappeared. In 2003, towel-maker giant Pillowtex filed for bankruptcy for the second time in three years and emptied its Kannapolis plant. Some 4,800 people were fired overnight—nearly one out of six people in town. Wise knits her brow, remembering. The job losses hammered both recent arrivals, who received no unemployment benefits, and long-time residents, who faced few alternatives for work. They waited years for unpaid vacation and severance.

Wise directs the Southeast Regional Economic Justice Network (REJN), which organized a project to address the rising racial tensions and bring Pillowtex workers together to demand accountability from local and state officials. Following the Imperial Foods fire, REJN had brought together twenty-five groups in an unprecedented coalition to win the passage of work-place safety reforms—then together block efforts to weaken worker compensation laws. REJN members, mainly organizations based throughout the South, serve low-wage workers, women and youth on an array of issues from education to workers' rights. They share resources, strategy, and experience through the network and pitch in on each other's campaigns, strengthening the push for social justice across the region.

Wise and two collaborators started REJN in 1989 when they realized that the South really was unlike anyplace else when it came to organizing. Very specific circumstances and realities set it apart from the rest of the nation. The legacy of slavery saturates every aspect of society. White people control most of the wealth, while black people are disproportionately poor and underrepresented in positions of power. An antilabor, antiregulation climate persists, helped along by powerful businesses that keep a strong hand in shaping government policy. From the outset REJN founders organized the network to address racial and ethnic power relations among their own groups. They have learned that in order to build a movement, they must forge trusting relationships and nurture individual wellness and self-esteem.

In leading this work, Wise weaves together a deep sense of the personal aspects of organizing as well as the historical realities. Tall and regal, she moves lightly and gracefully even though post-polio syndrome has slowed her walk and tires her easily. She knows when to be tough as steel and when to warm up a crowd with love. "She walks in a room and things light up," says Baldemar Velasquez, president of the Farm Labor Organizing Committee (FLOC). She spoke at a farmworker rally and in no time had everyone "all fired up and chanting," he remembers. "She's a spark."

When FLOC first moved its operations south from its U.S. headquarters in Ohio, REJN reached out. Wise connected Velasquez to African-American leaders throughout the region. She warned him of the deep divisions between black and white society and explained to him, "Organizing here is not like organizing in Ohio." Velasquez remembers, "It changed how I approached people."

One thing she preaches is "patience and thick skin," as Wise herself describes it. Her advice hit home one day when Velasquez found himself confronted by a white farmer, who was enraged that FLOC had signed up all his workers. "He came up, really angry, spewing all his (racial) venom. I had learned how to sit there and be quiet and ask if he was finished," Velasquez says. "You learn to expect that and let it bounce off your hide. By the end of the conversation, I had him half-convinced we were right." With REJN support, FLOC won an international union contract with the North Carolina Grower Association in 2004 that covered eight thousand legal guest workers growing twenty-seven crops on one thousand separate farms.

Raised in Berkeley, California, by politically active parents in an interracial marriage, Wise still trusts in the faith, cultural respect and dignity of labor they taught her. She grew up in a house with 30-foot antenna towers on the roof, listening to her father communicate on his ham radio and feeling connected to people around the world as she found their locations on a huge map on the wall.

The summer after she finished high school, Wise won a scholarship to a 70-hour symposium on dance technique and composition taught by Merce Cunningham. Then she headed off to Occidental College in Los Angeles, and next to Wisconsin to study under the famed foreign affairs historian William Appleton Williams. She became an expert in oral history and helped compile the Wisconsin Historical Society's extensive Civil Rights Collection. She joined the Concerned Black Students in Wisconsin, an affiliate of the Student Non-Violent Coordinating Committee, and two years later, she says, "married into" the SNCC family. By 1968 she had settled in Georgia as an archivist for the Martin Luther King Jr. Center for Non-Violent Social Change, which advances the legacy of Dr. King. In Atlanta, with its sizeable black community, she could go to the bank, shop in the grocery store, and carry out all the other activities of the day without seeing a single white person. "Where are all the white people?" she remembers wondering.

When her marriage ended she left for North Carolina and started graduate school at Duke University. Wise's ex-husband quit paying child support, so she had to find work. After more than three months of searching, she landed a job at a steel fabrication plant in Raleigh and earned certificates in arc welding and reading blueprints. It was 1977, and the locker rooms were segregated. Few workers, black or white, would look their white foreman in the eye. As one of three women among 350 men, Wise discovered firsthand the effects of having every step under suspicion. "You can't afford to make one mistake. Usually, once a day my whole time there, I'd hear, 'Why don't you get a woman's job?'"

Wise found herself for the first time in the middle of not just Southern culture, but Southern male culture, feeling "the combined degradation of race, class and gender bias," she recalls. The people she worked with barely knew who Dr. Martin Luther King Jr. was. They carried the weight of living each day as second-class citizens in their demeanor and often, their behavior as well. Their resignation and her own feeling of erosion in self-confidence were new to Wise, who just before had been working toward a master's degree. "I'd never regarded anybody as not my peer, even someone I respected highly," explains Wise, hand on her hip.

Now Wise recognizes the many ways suspicion built into interracial relations in the South leaks into and undermines organizing efforts. Since black people and white people typically don't socialize together, meetings must be held somewhere on neutral ground to discuss anything from county policy to workplace regulation. "Well, when [black] people don't speak to white people directly, it's a huge challenge," Wise points out wryly.

When Wise began planning REJN with Leroy Johnson and Bill Troy, she was directing Southerners for Economic Justice. She and Troy, an ordained minister, were associated with the Inter-religious Economic Crisis Organizing Network. She worked with Johnson for the Urban Rural Mission of the World Council of Churches. As they traveled around the world, they kept feeling the mirror turned upon their own situation in the South. In many ways, they felt more similarities with countries south of the U.S. border than with states above the Mason-Dixon line. In shaping REJN, they realized that a global economic analysis and international connections had to be part of their work. Today, REJN's members stretch from Canada to Ecuador.

The REJN founders absorbed other lessons from the international, faith-based work they had been doing. As Wise says, "Each saw organizing for justice as a spiritual discipline." Over the years REJN developed a philosophy of "transformational organizing," which Wise describes as going beyond the issues at hand to overcome fear, internalized racism, and Bible Belt homophobia. The approach binds efforts to change external policy with internal work such as elevating self-esteem, building relationships of trust, sharing leadership, and even tending to personal well-being. Building a movement, they believed, requires that people find pride in the work they do, that they learn to speak up on their own behalf, and that they begin to see themselves as deserving contributors to society. "By modeling just and caring community, we have found ways of stretching folk without alienating them," Wise explains.

They found that getting people to collaborate on campaigns also was not as simple as it sounds. The process takes plenty of trial and error, and every new group presents a fresh challenge. When injured workers first joined the network, for instance, other participants had to become more conscious about things like wearing perfumes, taking more breaks, and making access easy. Wise realized she needed help teaching people to communicate across buried fears and hostility, too, so she turned to an Urban Rural Mission colleague and Mi'kmaq healer from New Brunswick, Canada. Joanne Bartibogue, a member of the Wabanaki Nation, came and taught the traditions of smudging and women's healing circles.

Sometimes barriers disappear in unplanned ways. One day, during a gathering that included injured workers, a massage therapist offered to soothe their necks and shoulders. Before she touched anyone, she told the group, she would stand quietly behind that person for a moment to greet and honor his or her spirit. The gesture, especially by a woman who was white, affected many of them deeply. "For some of these folks, black workers who had never had a peer relationship with a white person, ever, and who had never had a white person honor them, it was a breakthrough," Wise recalls. "People started to open up."

A former performer with the Chuck Davis African American Dance Ensemble, Wise also has helped REJN build time into its sessions for practices such as dance, drumming and meditation. Wise has found that foundation executives' eyes glaze over at words like "spirituality" and "healing," and when she became more open about REJN's efforts, it lost some funding. But in the South, faith feeds people in their day-to-day struggle to put food on the table, raise their families, and live with dignity. By tapping into body and spirit, participants not only find their own inner strength, but also develop the physical and emotional trust necessary to work together under trying circumstances.

In one core effort, REJN has focused on building relationships between black people and Latino immigrants, in part to address perceptions that one group is responsible for the challenges faced by the other. REJN organizers could see that farmworkers and factory workers, immigrants and African-Americans across the region could together demand better working conditions and help for people who had lost their livelihoods. But trust and understanding had to come first. After Pillowtex closed, the immigrants at the North Carolina factory weren't entitled to benefits. But many of those who stayed in town found work cleaning hotel rooms, doing yard jobs or painting houses. The black people on the looms at Pillowtex—many of whom had not finished high school—felt the Latinos were taking opportunities that would have gone to them before.

Wise got in touch with African diaspora expert and photographer Ron Wilkins, an old friend from SNCC who specializes in building cross-cultural peace between Mexicans and African-Americans. In his studies and work-shops, he brings together images and history that show the longstanding inter-dependence between conquered indigenous populations and once enslaved Africans in Mexico. In one series of photos, he features villagers of African ancestry from the Oaxacan coast.

Wilkins had already come to North Carolina four years before at Wise's invitation. He remembers that she talked him into shipping his twenty-five-piece exhibit to her so she could take it on the road. One place she set it up was St. Joseph Catholic Church, in Cabarrus County, where Latino and black workers from Pillowtex lived. The images show families and friends together, some with black features, some who look more indigenous, and some who seem a clear blend. In one picture titled "Playmates," two little Afro-Mexican girls, one with black features and one with indigenous ones, hold hands and smile brightly. They are niece and aunt to each other. Another group of children sport a mixture of straight and curly hair, dark skin and lighter, modern clothes and embroidered village blouses.

"We have mutual interests and we even share ancestors," Wilkins says, referring to the historical amnesia that cuts black people off from themselves. He has seen the combination of images and black-brown history stir people to discard nativist attitudes and begin to see their own history differently.

REJN has found other ways to bring black and brown together, too. In a community forum held in Benson, North Carolina, a year earlier, organizers split participants in groups of three and four. Then African-Americans and Latinos simply shared their life experiences and asked each other questions. What do you eat? How do you cook? What do you miss about not being home? One young woman told her group that she wished she could have gone home to her mother's funeral in Mexico. "What I miss here most is my liberty," said another, describing how she lives in fear of being picked up by immigration police. The exchange reminded black and brown workers how much they shared. "Tears were coming to people's eyes," Wise remembers. "It just kind of broke through a lot of stuff."

Jose Montenegro

"Most of us had no choice, had left Mexico even though
we wanted to stay."

Out the kitchen door of his childhood home in Providencia, Mexico, Jose Montenegro could see a soaring mountain, its ridges dusted with dark green Ponderosa pine. He could walk down the dirt road at its foot, watching the wild sunflowers turn their brown and yellow faces to the light. "Just the scent of the rain, I will never forget," he says dreamily.

For the past sixteen years, Montenegro has been on a journey to recover that mountain, those sunflowers, and the rain. Like many other immigrants to the United States, his identity, culture, and ancestry seemed to vanish when he crossed the border. At twenty-three he became a low-wage worker, an outsider, a problem instead of a person. He lived in the shadow of U.S. society. And while eventually he found a good job and raised a family here, he could never shake the feeling that he had left something important behind. "For many years I tried to go to Providencia, pull up these roots and plant them here, but I realized I had only branches," he says, recalling his futile efforts to transplant who he was.

Drawing from this sense of loss, Montenegro has developed a series of programs to help Latinos build a healthier relationship with the new society they live in. For nine years he walked Salinas Valley fields with California farm workers, teaching them to become independent farmers. Later he began training forest laborers in the Northwest to speak up for themselves and participate in forestry management decisions. Instead of being viewed and treated as objects, he says, immigrants should be free to shape their own lives. At the core, Montenegro wants to enable them to reconnect with the land they left behind, and in doing so, reconnect with their own hearts.

Montenegro began this work out of the Rural Development Center in Salinas, California, in 1993, eight years after its founding by the Association for Community-Based Education (ACBE) in Washington, D.C. When he first developed the program for new farmers, Florentino Collazo was just the sort of person he had in mind. Collazo had left his family's forty-acre ranch in Mexico more than a decade before to cut and pack lettuce in the Salinas Valley. He worked hard and was promoted to foreman. But where he came from, life on the land meant more than toiling among identical rows of lettuce and connecting irrigation pipe. And while the vegetables he helped grow looked beautiful, he knew they were loaded with chemical fertilizers and pesticides.

Collazo opens his broad hands, remembering the constant rashes. Always in the back of his mind, he was thinking, "Where? How? When?"

The answer came on a local cable television show. Collazo heard Montenegro describing the center's six-month course, which teaches the process of organic farming from seed to sale, from distribution to accounting, and enrolled. After graduation he signed up for the center's three-year farm incubation period, leasing a plot of land and receiving technical assistance, equipment, and water as part of the package. More than five hundred families or individuals have taken the center's classes, which are conducted in Spanish, and of those, about three-quarters have struck out on their own.

Now Collazo has taken over management of the 112-acre farming operation where the training takes place, encouraging new farmers, helping them set up irrigation schedules, and giving them a hand with their equipment. He stands on hard, brown dirt beneath a Bishop pine, hands thrust in a black corduroy jacket over a plaid burgundy flannel shirt. The Rural Development Center's shop, training center, and a small white farmhouse sit solidly around him. Long rows sprouting leafy greens and strawberries stretch neatly beyond.

Collazo walks out to a chest-high cover crop of vetch, bellbeans, magnus peas, and oats, with a small, chocolate-copper dog named Tomasa trotting alongside. The birds above chatter so loudly that they almost drown the man out. He reaches over and plucks a black-and-white flower from a vine. "Before, I was a robot. Every day it was the same job," he says. "Here, it's a rainbow."

Montenegro had hoped to help immigrants learn more than how to grow crops; he wanted them to tap into the feeling of independence and ownership that comes with farm life. His students came from peasant families that had ranched or grown row crops for generations. "Most of us had no choice, had left Mexico even though we wanted to stay," Montenegro says. "Here at this program, we found a space where we could tell our stories, talk about our struggles and our aspirations."

Montenegro calls immigration from Mexico and Latin America a "forced migration" created by new land policies in Mexico, the North American Free Trade Agreement (NAFTA), and U.S. food dumping. He himself left behind a family farm where his father still cultivates corn and beans, but there is no market for what he grows. Montenegro studied agronomy in college, but did not want to take a government job with priorities that seemed to betray his own kin.

With no other choice, Montenegro waved good-bye to his parents late that summer through the dusty window of an old bus, the image of his little village lingering along with the sadness he felt. He eventually arrived in Chicago at the home of relatives who had settled there, and within a week, his uncle found him a job unloading trailers. "It was awful," he says. He quit in no time and took off for Milwaukee, where cousins on his father's side lived. They met him in the community plaza, then told him they had no room to take him in. While he stood reeling from the news, the people around him celebrated Mexican Independence Day. Finally a familiar face approached and asked where he was from. He turned out to be a childhood friend offering to help.

The friend gave him a place to stay, and eventually he found a job on the night shift at a foundry. But the tasks were boring, and the sound of machinery pounded incessantly into his head. "One day, I was working in the morning, sweeping the floor," he recalls. "I stopped for a split second and the foreman prodded my shoulder, 'Why do you stop?'

"I just threw the broom down."

His young wife, Maggie, picked him up from the factory; after he told her what happened, he began to cry. "I didn't know how to deal with the physical, the spiritual separation from my geography," Montenegro tries to explain. "Something had happened to me when I crossed the border, deeply, internally, and I was trying to put the pieces together." Montenegro bounced through a couple more jobs—as a teacher's assistant, then a car salesman— before he told Maggie he thought they should go to California, where he could find work in agriculture. But when he got to the West Coast, he still felt lost. That's when Maggie happened across the ad placed by the Rural Development Center for a farm manager and educator.

Finally, Montenegro had found his place. He worked among dozens of immigrants like himself, people like his father, who plowed the land. He gave classes and ran the farm, becoming director of the whole program after two years. He knew right away that the project had to reach beyond seeds and tillage to recreate the feeling of community that immigrants had lost. But where were the women? The children? He thought about it and realized that with its pesticides and fertilizers, the area wasn't safe for farm families. "That started the revolution," he says now, with a snap of his fingers.

Two acres of the center had already been certified organic. Montenegro learned everything he could about sustainable farming and began transitioning the rest. Students embraced the new idea. They recalled the Green Revolution, which brought hybrid grains and high-input agriculture to developing countries starting in the late 1940s. While the new farming practices boosted productivity, they cost the land and the people their health. Organic approaches seemed a way to reconnect to an ancestral way of living on the land. "Then the women and children started to come," Montenegro recalls with a smile.

By then, resource conservationist Daniel Mountjoy had become a regular fixture at the center, teaching farmers about soil and water and helping to install hedgerows and windbreaks. "I was really inspired by the way Jose crafted his programs in a culturally appropriate way," Mountjoy says. Instead of sitting everyone down and lecturing at them, Montenegro would ask questions and draw pictures on a flipchart. What did they value in the environment? He'd draw a picture of a fish. Then he would show how pesticides drained into the creeks, streams, and Monterey Bay. "He'd always tie things together in ways that made sense to the farmers. He'd show the relationships between ideas and practices, implements and climate," Mountjoy observes.

Mountjoy also had been working with Latinos already established on small farms in the Elkhorn Slough area north of Salinas. In a three-way brainstorming session, he, Montenegro, and the manager of the Elkhorn Resource Conservation District decided that the Rural Development Center ought to extend its training there. Mountjoy found a 180-acre parcel slated to be developed into high-end homes, and the three began to negotiate, push, prod, and plea. Local environmentalists didn't support any kind of farming in the watershed because they wanted it to revert to natural habitat. Hearing their skepticism, some Latinos sensed racism. It was a tense time, but Montenegro kept the group focused. "He was very level-headed, a visionary. He was such a great partner," Mountjoy says.

In the end, the team convinced environmentalists that the Rural Development Center had an admirable track record turning farmers with barely any education into passionate environmental stewards. The Elkhorn Slough Foundation bought the conservation easement to the land and the Packard Foundation paid for the rest. The center began to restore native vegetation on the hillsides and put in features for erosion control. Farmers began to try out organic practices and conservation techniques on the tillable land. "They've gone on to be the primary outreach project for conservation in the area, as anticipated," points out Mountjoy, who is now assistant state conservationist for the agency.

But still Montenegro wasn't satisfied. "Even though we had access to these wonderful resources, we kept talking about our roots. People kept talking about mi tierra, my land back home, my adobe house. How can I be me without my oak tree?" Montenegro asks. The question had followed him since the moment he boarded that dusty bus.

Montenegro thought of creating a binational exchange project in which people living in the United States and Mexico could trade not only ideas and resources about farming but also this feeling of connection to the land. The program would give migrants an opportunity to return, at least in spirit. He had pressed his Washington managers to let the Rural Development Center move into local hands, which they did, at the cost of his job. So he gathered a board, found new funding, and created El Centro Internacional para el Desarrollo Rural Sostenible (CIDERS), or the International Center for Sustainable Rural Development.

Working with grassroots organizations in Mexico, Montenegro invited farmers and the children of farmers from rural areas to propose their own curriculum, centered on a community project that would help them stay on the land. They asked for topics from forest restoration to ecological architecture. In the United States Montenegro began working with the Latino immigrants who gathered brush, replanted trees, made cedar shakes, and fought fires on national and private forest lands in Oregon and Washington. Montenegro had hoped they would participate in binational exchanges, but first the foresters wanted something else. "They said, 'Jose, great idea, but we are here. We have so many problems here,'" Montenegro recalls.

They labored in fast-paced, dangerous conditions by day and slept at night in tattered tents. Working with the Pacific West Community Forestry Center and the Jefferson Center, Montenegro began helping the forest workers and harvesters develop leadership skills. Together they came up with a plan for two-day annual forums in which they could share stories and ideas, music and food. Montenegro had come to believe that immigrants need more than economic and educational access. They also must have the opportunity to reflect on who they are, where they come from, and their values and vision for the future. "So much of what he did was helping people recover who they are, recover their identity," says Katie Bagby, coordinator for the Pacific West center. "Watching him lead and empower people was wonderful to see."

The immigrants began to analyze and research trends in economics, immigration, and forestry management in order to negotiate better wages, safer practices, and reasonable living conditions. Foresters from Shelton, Washington, started to meet regularly, creating the Grupo de Trabajadores Hispanos. They sat down with forest officials and participated in local government meetings. They pressed for health care, education, and credit.

Montenegro ran CIDERS for three years, but with Maggie back in college, two teenagers needing attention, and a four-year-old son, the travel had become unbearable for his family. Home in Salinas, Montenegro had decided he needed a better foundation for the work he wanted to do. The master's program in public policy at California State University, Monterey Bay, gave him that opportunity. "This program is helping me make sense of things I didn't understand when I left Mexico," he explains. "Why is it that my father, and thousands of farmers like him, cannot be successful?" He is beginning to understand the structural reasons and to envision ways to solve them.

Montenegro doesn't yet have all the answers, but he does have one idea. He thinks back to a sixty-acre piece of forestland that has been in his family for a couple of generations. Montenegro convinced his aunts to sell their shares to him in order to preserve it for the community. He dreams of bringing children there to learn about biodiversity, to discover the plants and animals of the forest. College students and the children of farmers might also participate in a resident program to study forest restoration and ecological architecture. "Hopefully, we'd be able to develop a long-term vision. Block by block, we would develop a foundation before it's too late," he says. Instead of sending their children to the United States, families who live on the land would have the resources to thrive in Mexico. "Many young people do not aspire to leave their place and immigrate," he points out wryly.

But Montenegro doesn't plan to return to Providencia and settle in. Instead he will live part of the year in Mexico, part in California. Through his work in the fields and the forests, with the people who have traveled the same long distance he has, he has found a way home. He has roots in both lands now.

Janet Robideau

"We really came out like gangbusters. But at the time, that's what we had to do."

In Billings, Montana a few years ago, a group of skinheads tried to make Pioneer Park whites-only. In Bozeman, flyers all over town claimed that government policies to create a "Third World America" were costing white children their futures. In response to incidents such as these, whole communities in Montana have gathered to march against hate crimes. But when a YWCA television ad recently asked people to think about whether racism exists in the state, viewers called the agency in anger. For many Montanans, the "R-word" is offensive in itself. They will tell you that only extremists think in an R-word way

Janet Robideau, however, has no doubt racism exists — both overt and otherwise — and she's not afraid to say so. She sees evidence of it every day in the dropout rate of American Indian schoolchildren, which is three times that of white kids, and in school textbooks that barely mention Native Americans. She finds it in the poor emergency response times into Indian neighborhoods and in a police scanner broadcast she once heard that warned of a drinking and crime spree "now that Indians got their checks" for the month. She feels it when shopkeepers make degrading comments to Indians, such as asking whether they can really afford the goods they are buying. "Racism is this huge elephant in the middle of the room," Robideau says. "People hide their faces; they walk over it and under it." About Indian People's Action (IPA), the group she founded in 1997, she says, "We go around and say, 'Look! There's this elephant in the room. It's huge! We have to get it out of here together.'"

Robideau may gently use a joke to show people the reality of racism, or she may pound her fist on the table and demand that they see it. Under her guidance, IPA and its five hundred members have challenged disparate treatment of Indians and non-Indians by school districts, law enforcement, and the healthcare system. They have picketed the governor's office and shown up in force to accuse police officers of discrimination. In the beginning, says Robideau, "We really came out like gangbusters." She later apologized to the governor for the group's unrelenting pressure. "But at the time, that was what we had to do."

IPA, a chapter of Montana People's Action (MPA) based in Missoula, is one of only a few — but growing number of — organizations in the country that advocates for urban Indians. The concessions its members have achieved, such as a voice in the school curriculum and changes in school and law-enforcement hiring practices, have become the foundation for ongoing and lasting change. After more than a decade the group finds that local agencies have stopped looking at them as complaining Indians and now take their concerns more seriously. After they butted heads with the police, the sheriff called and asked how his department could avoid being next.

Robideau walks slowly and with effort because of her rheumatoid arthritis. She wears her curly coffee-colored hair with a tint of red, and she keeps her fingernails long and painted dark burgundy. It can be hard to imagine her squaring off against a cop as she nuzzles and plays gently with her basset hound, Sadie, who is standing atop the picnic table behind her cozy new house. Robideau points to her totem, the grizzly. Intelligent and fierce, this animal also likes to wrestle and frolic. "I can be intimidating or I can be playful — you choose," Robideau explains. The bear's image is everywhere, from the five-foot statue wearing a red "Organize" T-shirt in the corner of her office to the large, fearsome claw print on the top of her filing cabinet. There's a bear cookie jar on the counter of her bright mustard-yellow kitchen and a

Robideau points to her totem, the grizzly. Intelligent and fierce, this
animal also likes to wrestle and frolic. "I can be intimidating or I can
be playful—you choose," Robideau explains.

more natural-looking sculpted creature peering down from a nook above the hallway that leads to the bedrooms.

A huge bag of bubblegum dominates the small kitchen island and serves as another kind of totem for Robideau. It's a sort of mutinous reminder of government and Catholic boarding schools she endured as a youth. "They weren't exactly nice," Robideau says bitterly, remembering the teachers and nuns. The schools operated under a harsh principle of cultural and linguistic assimilation. Physical punishment was routine. If she was caught chewing gum, Robideau had to stand on her tiptoes with her nose touching the inside of a circle drawn high on the blackboard. Then the teacher would hit the back of her legs with a stick. The nuns would make the children kneel bare-kneed on a broomstick, she recalls. To this day Robideau won't touch oatmeal, the runny breakfast glop she got every morning. She sleeps in as often as possible, remembering the six AM wake-up for mass a half hour later. In high school she organized a dorm council to have a say in work distribution and to ask for events like dorm parties. "The thing that angered me most is they'd always say no — and they'd never tell me why," she says. "That is the basis for why I organize."

When Robideau graduated from high school in 1969, she stayed on the Northern Cheyenne Reservation, where she and her mother had moved nearly ten years earlier to be with her grandparents. By then the rage planted and cultivated by the schools had become central to who she was. She tried to swallow her feelings by drinking alcohol, but they spilled out in bouts of fury. "I would break windows," she remembers. At about that time members of the American Indian Movement (AIM), which got its start inside the prisons of the Midwest, were returning to their impoverished home reservations and reacting with shock. As Robideau watched them challenge corruption, violence, and police brutality, she was amazed and heartened. She married into the movement and joined the fight for change, letting her simmering anger fuel her. After the AIM occupation and standoff against armed federal officials at Wounded Knee in 1973, she returned to her birthplace in the San Francisco Bay Area and got a job at the InterTribal Friendship House. For the first time, she had seen Native Americans fight back against oppression. "I got to see how Indian people could work together," she says.

Robideau didn't stay long, though, moving back to Montana with her young daughter. By then she was in her late twenties and, after a few boring years as a clerk with the state highway department, she decided to return to school. At the university, one professor looked at her skin tone and facial features and told her she'd have a hard time earning a degree. She summoned all her patience not to respond or walk out and eventually achieved both a bachelor's and master's degree in psychology. Her studies gave her insight into others as well as herself. She learned to look for what people held in their hearts instead of latching onto something stupid they might say. She also began to learn about her own anger and how to transform it into a powerful instrument instead of a destructive force.

Robideau's first organizing effort as an adult came after she graduated in her late thirties, when she went to work as a nursing assistant and discovered how poorly both workers and residents were treated. She helped organize a union and pushed for resident rights. Later she joined Montana People's Action, which brings together low- and moderate-income residents on healthcare issues, living wages, and affordable housing. The director, Jim Fleishmann, encouraged and coached her. "He taught me I could fight with people and not stay mad till the end of time," Robideau remembers. She says he would tell her, "Let's take that hot anger and turn it into a cold anger and make it useful." She realized that this was the kind of work she wanted to do for the rest of her life.

In 1996 she convinced Fleishmann to create a statewide chapter to focus on the needs of urban Indians, who were largely invisible in society. It took a year to find funding and longer to lure members. Robideau knocked on doors — more than six hundred in Missoula alone, she recalls — went to

Indian Center meetings, and nabbed lists of names when she could. One of her challenges has been to convince Indian people to want to work with non-Indians and to build trust in both directions. Even within the organization she must try to prepare different cultures for one another. It doesn't always work out perfectly, but she says, "I just remember something my mother said — it's human nature, they'll let you down. You have to trust Creator. That's the only person who will never let you down." Indeed, her traditional beliefs help guide her and give her strength, "and give me someone to get mad at when things go wrong," she adds with a laugh.

Over time Robideau has learned to see why people hang onto hateful attitudes toward one another and how to address their underlying fears. She has discovered how to avoid defensive reactions and unnecessary battles and how to use confrontation more effectively. Robideau now uses her schooling and experience in a process called "dismantling racism," which is designed to move beyond feel-good discussions of multiculturalism and tolerance. This approach, used by the Western States Center and other progressive organizations, aims to break down the foundations of racial injustice. The training addresses the stereotypes people hold about others and the ones we hold about ourselves, then it goes deeper. The work gets to the core of white privilege, power relations, and a social system with racism at its historical center. "It's pretty harsh training," Robideau says. "It's not how to respond when someone makes a joke about another person's religion. It's reaching in, grabbing your heart, showing it to you, and putting it back in you." Racism is really based on ignorance, she says, and the ideas that people silently hold about one another. In order to change our secret belief systems, she says, "You have to dig in and dig deep."

At local agencies and schools, IPA goes after the racism built into attitudes and policies. In a meeting with supervisory police officers in fall of 2000, one hundred people turned out and, one after another, told their stories of racial profiling. Missoula City Police Chief Rusty Wickman, who was a lieutenant at the time, remembers how awful that first meeting felt. But after the air cleared and the police department instituted Native American–specific, anti-racism training for the entire staff, "things became really good," he says. "We have come to be advocates of one another." Both sides learned how they might have misinterpreted the other's culture. Indian youth are taught not to look adults in the eye, for instance, but police are taught that looking down or away is probably a sign of guilt. Now, Wickman knows, "If an urban Indian doesn't want to look you in the eye, it may mean that he doesn't want to disrespect you."

IPA joined the police in marches in 2002 when the officers' union was seeking a better contract, and Wickman's predecessor volunteered to join Robideau as a target for a whipped-cream pie toss in an MPA anniversary celebration. The department hired its first Native American officer in 2000 and made it easier for American Indians to complain about officer conduct. "Janet is one of my favorite people," says Wickman. "She's quite a force and has common sense, too. She's fair."

IPA also has participated in a nationwide data analysis of race-based disparities in schools and several years ago gave the Missoula County Public School District a very public grade of "F." The "racial justice report card" analyzed trends such as high dropout rates, a lack of diversity on staff, and disparities in disciplining American Indians, who in Missoula make up about 5 percent of the student population. The chair of the school board complained to the newspaper that he and his colleagues had already spent two years working with the group and had "bent over backward to address their problems." But the district soon became the first in Montana to enact a thirty-year-old state mandate to recognize Native American culture and heritage in the curriculum.

Robideau says the school campaign has been an especially effective means of getting Montana's urban Indians involved in social activism. When she tries to recruit members by talking about racial profiling and discrimination, many Indians just shrug their shoulders. "People say, 'That's not us, we don't protest,'" she explains, characterizing their attitude. But when it comes to their children, it's another issue entirely. "'If you harm my children, God help you, I'll take you out,'" she warns, playing the role. "Our job is to make this place better for those who come behind." At IPA's annual Indian Taco Sale fundraiser on Columbus Day, several generations turn out, including Robideau's thirty-four-year-old daughter, Francine, and many others who consider Robideau family.

As the scent of garlic, onions, chili powder, and hamburger being pre-pared in the kitchen wafted around her, Robideau rested a minute at one of the tables. She told her friend Francena Gamboa that she wanted to dye her hair blonde and shape it into a spike, but Gamboa was having none of it. "Those girls over there, she gave them a vision," Gamboa said, pointing to her own daughter and niece, who are both active in the Gay-Straight Alliance in high school. "My sister back there in the kitchen — she takes what she learned back to work. Janet's not telling us what to do. She's telling us what we all *can* do."

In the early days, IPA came out tough and hot on issues. " I say we had to throw the school district against the wall to get them to listen. We did the same with the cops," Robideau remembers. But public confrontation may be less necessary now. MPA and IPA recently issued a report on brutality and mis-conduct on the part of Billings police officers. The groups, both now directed by Robideau, are asking for a community review board, more minorities on the staff, and antiracism training. They're meeting with resistance, Robideau says, but perhaps this time the groups won't have to picket and shout. Even as they push people, Robideau says, they plan to keep the anger cool and care-fully applied. "Now I say, let's use the *threat* of the sledgehammer."

Kathy Goldman

"Tomorrow morning, if the will were there, we would not
have to have any hunger. There is no dearth of food."

Sandra Ramos, Joseph McCoy, and their fellow students were silent for a
moment as they contemplated the bounty of their own efforts: Styrofoam
plates heaped with waffles and fruit-filled crepes. Omelets, bacon, and toast,
and noodles topped with grated cheese. Berries and sliced melon mounded
in every spare bit of space. A small cup of pea soup teetering on the side.

They ate every bite—and a few had seconds.

The generous spread was the morning's work of the Community Food
Resource Center's Culinary Training Program: a ten-week, full-time training
seminar for fourteen future food-service chefs. While the group turned back
to its lessons in the dining room, activity started up in the kitchen for the
evening meal. Men and women in white smocks and blue "Community
Kitchen" hats moved among the gleaming stoves and massive kettles, preparing Italian turkey sausage, ravioli, and green peas for the free dinner.

The central Harlem storefront was serving more than 550 meals every day
in sit-down dinners, home deliveries, and take-out packs. "It's very intense
stuff. You have to perform," said Kathy Goldman, founder and former executive director. "If we didn't serve one night, it'd be a disaster for hundreds of

people." As she watched the chefs-in-training buzz around the kitchen that day, Goldman admitted, "It's terrifying."

Goldman, always with an idea in her trousers' pockets and a plan in her head, isn't easily intimidated. For four decades, she has insisted that everyone in New York City has a right to food on the table. She has pressed recalcitrant city council members for attention and corporate-minded funders for money. She has built a thriving food service and advocacy organization from the ground up.

Driven by an acute awareness of the ongoing, pressing need, she has barely eased up for a moment. In New York City, which has a poverty rate nearly twice the national average, hunger keeps growing. One in seven New Yorkers can't count on regular meals. Only about half of those eligible for food stamps are getting them. "When I stop to think about it, I get very depressed," Goldman says. "People are living in the most awful conditions."

What's more, Goldman knows food is a solvable problem. She will look you right in the eye and tell you straight: "Tomorrow morning if the will were there, we would not have to have any hunger. There's no dearth of food."

The child of Hungarian immigrants, Goldman grew up in the Bronx, immersed in communist ideals. Her father was a carpenter and union organizer; her mother wrote humor columns for an immigrant newspaper. She became political herself by necessity when she was in the first—mostly unwelcome—class of girls allowed into the Bronx High School of Science in 1946. Later she joined the Labor Youth League, and in the early 1950s, as a newlywed and then young mother, she typed transcripts all night long for witnesses hauled before the House Un-American Activities Committee.

Food was central to the family culture, as well as to friendship and politics. "Many, many years ago, in the '60s, I discovered that food means a great deal to people," Goldman says. Even today her grandchildren always ask for the story of "meatloaf surprise," her own specialty with a hard-boiled egg and a hotdog hidden inside.

Friends say Goldman's mission to feed New York City got started when organizer, radical, and now best buddy, Jesse Cagan, plucked a pregnant Goldman out of a PTA meeting. Cagan asked Goldman to join a group that

*"It hit me—how important food was.
I just stayed with it the rest of my life."*

was organizing to improve public schools, especially to challenge race-based inequities.

There were many issues that needed attention, but Latino and black parents in the South Bronx put the schools' inedible cafeteria lunches at the top of their lists. With family resources stretched to the limit, they needed to know that they could rely on the school to provide their children with one good meal every day. "That meal for their kids was so vital, so critical, that when there was a problem with it, it became a major financial problem for the family," she says. "It hit me—how important food was. I just stayed with it the rest of my life."

The school meals tasted terrible and were dangerous, too. In one cafeteria there was no hot water or any scouring powder. Goldman quickly got action from stubborn school administrators. Without letting on where they were going, she invited all the local elected officials to lunch—in the school cafeteria. "Thank God one of the assemblymen got sick on the food. It was just perfect. It caused a riot," Goldman says, and pauses in thought. "You know, you can have a lot of fun organizing."

Food proved to be an excellent organizing tool, too. Poor parents back then would accept being told their children were stupid. They'd let teachers wave away questions about why their sons or daughters couldn't read. But as one of them stood up and told the Board of Education in 1968, "On food and sex, you can't tell me a thing." They had lots of ideas about how to replace frozen "meal packs" with something more edible and nutritious. As Goldman clearly loves to recall, fifty women showed up for a meeting to decide on just the right mix of spices for chicken and rice.

School lunches got better and Goldman began pushing for meals during the summer break; in 1971 she finally convinced New York State to take advantage of a federal program that paid for 250,000 lunches daily at 1,000 community sites. She began working on long-term policy, leading a drive for school breakfasts as well. By 1976 the state legislature had passed a law requiring morning meals at schools in the five largest cities in New York State.

In 1980 Goldman founded the Community Food Resource Center (CFRC). She aimed to get more people connected to existing programs, such as food stamps, school breakfasts and lunches, child care, and senior meals. The center opened up offices in a tiny tenement building and quickly began taking over more floors. Projects expanded to include eviction prevention, media advocacy, public speaking training, and Food Force, a team of advisors who fanned out around the city each day to help people apply for food stamps. The center set up tax offices to help people collect their earned income tax credit, which can run to nearly $6,000 for a family with two children. "A lot of it just happened because Kathy had an idea," said nutritionist Agnes Molnar, who has worked with Goldman for more than twenty-five years. "She dreams up these schemes all the time."

When Goldman realized that public grade-school cafeterias were sitting empty every afternoon, she began pressing for dinner service for older people. The dinner clients asked for activities, too, so dancing and movies joined the schedule. On the day program director Pat Caldwell turned seventy, the group at Public School 134 in lower Manhattan celebrated with dinner, cake, a professional dance troupe of septuagenarians, and "Happy Birthday" sung in English, Spanish, and Mandarin. Goldman, black fanny pack at her waist, made a quick speech, cleaned up a spill, propped open a problem door, and joined in the dancing herself.

There have been some disasters and some plans that would have worked but for cost and effort. A drive to bring a huge Pathmark supermarket into a poverty-stricken area succeeded, but only after an all-absorbing and risky battle. An effort to get community groups to take on child nutrition flopped: drug prevention, sex education, and other issues already overwhelmed them. And there were the cherry tomatoes, a clever but, as it turned out, unworkable solution to the complicated problem of cutting big beefsteaks for salads in school lunches. "My phone . . . every principal. . . ." Goldman remembers. "I had not thought of them as missiles."

Goldman also had not imagined how difficult it would be to let go of her large enterprise when the huge administrative and fundraising burden became too much. In the last few years she ran CFRC, it employed about one hundred people and had a $7 million budget. In preparation for retirement, she set up internal programs such as in-house political training and clearer promotional opportunities. She identified her own successor, Richard Murphy, a friend and former youth commissioner for New York City, and spent a year talking him into the job. But when Murphy came on, she bridled at his approach. He began consolidating programs and required each one to pay for itself. He overhauled CFRC's image and renamed it FoodChange. He heightened financial accountability and cut out compensatory time off for overtime work. He redid the office with more businesslike touches and forbade workers from eating lunch at their desks.

Goldman had decided to remain on staff as program manager to ease the transition. After one miserable year, she left in frustration. Yet, according to Fran Barrett, a board member who has remained a close friend of Goldman's, Murphy brought in the kind of nonprofit culture that today's funders expect. Foundations want corporate-like practices, not the activist management style. "It's the crystallization of what's happening in nonprofits everywhere," Barrett explains. "Kathy was all about program—those days are over."

Murphy left four years later, while FoodChange has continued to grow. In 2006, the organization helped forty-four thousand families collect tax credits. It has expanded food programs into more than one hundred public schools. The entitlement clinic reaches beyond housing into other social services, and a financial education arm encourages savings accounts with matched funds. Nutrition education efforts teach elders, food-stamp recipients and school-age youth about healthy foods, and "crop-share" programs help create demand for locally grown fruits and vegetables.

Goldman has found renewed optimism back on the streets. She and her long-time friend and collaborator Agnes Molnar now share a job at the Children's Defense Fund, where they continue to work on food issues. They press for free meals for all children and better use of existing programs such as summer meals and school breakfasts. They meet with high school principals, monitor school cafeterias, and make suggestions. At one high school, for example, they offered this proposal: instead of requiring students to trundle up to the sixth floor every morning for their free breakfasts, why not let each student pick up a paper bag at one of the three building entrances?

When she was a young mother, Goldman believed change was around the corner. As she neared seventy, with a close-cropped crown of white, she concluded that it probably wouldn't happen while she was well and alive. Suddenly, though, New York City has begun to put food vulnerabilities center stage. "They're realizing that federal money is available and that it's an immediate boost to the economy," Goldman says.

The city council's most influential member successfully pressed for creating a citywide Food Policy Coordinator, something Goldman proposed back in 1979 with the thought of making hunger as central to government as roads and housing. Council members have eased the process to sign up for food stamps and held hearings on summer food programs for youth. A new breed of principals seems to be paying attention to the whole child, Goldman has noticed. With strict testing requirements, she thinks, they want to make sure everyone has a full stomach to propel learning.

It's painful to let go of the organization she started, especially because its emphasis and approach has shifted in ways Goldman finds hard to accept. But Food Change continues to raise money and expand in ways that will get more resources to needy New Yorkers. And after years of pressing city bureaucrats to recognize everyone's basic right to eat, Goldman is finally starting to see it happen. At seventy-five, she says she's thinking of "really retiring." But so far she stays deeply involved, still in the thick of the action, pacing the council hallways and checking out the cafeterias, demanding nutritious food for all New Yorkers and sensible strategies to get it to them. And now, powerful people are listening. "We give them a suggestion and they take it," Goldman marvels. "Of all the strange things to happen at this time of my life—the school system has agreed that children should have breakfast!"

Windcall Resident Program
Residents, 1989-2005

1989

Anthony Thigpenn, AGENDA/SCOPE, Los Angeles, CA

1990

Karen Fant, Washington Wilderness Coalition Executive Director, Seattle, WA

Margot Gibney, Encampment for Citizenship Executive Director, Berkeley, CA (now with Youth Treatment and Education Center, San Francisco, CA)

Roma Guy, The Women's Foundation Executive Director, San Francisco, CA (now with Bay Area Homelessness Program/CHHS/San Francisco State University, San Francisco, CA)

Davis Ja, PhD, Asian-American Recovery Services Executive Director, San Francisco, CA (now with Alliant University, Alameda, CA)

Mac Legerton, Center for Community Action, Lumberton, NC

Jonathan Polansky, Public Media Center, San Francisco, CA

Gary Sandusky, Idaho Citizens Network Executive Director, Boise, ID (now with Center for Community Change, Boise, ID)

Allan Solomonow, American Friends Service Committee–Middle East Program, San Francisco, CA

Dagmar Thorpe, Seventh Generation Fund Executive Director (now with Life-Way, Prague, OK)

Kathy Tyler, McAuley Institute Housing Development Specialist, Washington, DC (now with Motivation Education and Training, Inc., Austin, TX)

Robert "Woody" Widrow, National Housing Institute–Shelterforce Editor-in-Chief, Washington, DC (now in Austin, TX)

1991

Peter Barnes, Working Assets Funding Service President, San Francisco, CA (now with The Mesa Refuge and the Tomales Bay Institute, Point Reyes, CA)

Elizabeth Ainsley Campbell, CarEth Foundation Executive Director (now with Nashua River Watershed, Lunenberg, MA)

Victor Clark Alfaro, Binational Center for Human Rights/Centro Binacional de Derechos Humanos, Rio Tijuana, Tijuana, B.C. MEXICO

Bruce Gagnon, Florida Coalition for Peace and Justice, Gainesville, FL (now with Global Network Against Weapons and Nuclear Power in Space, Brunswick, ME)

David Hartsough, American Friends Service Committee, San Francisco, CA (now with Peaceworkers/Nonviolent Peaceforce, San Francisco, CA)

Clifford Honicker, Center for Clean Products and Clean Technology, Knoxville, TN (now with American Environmental Health Studies Project, Knoxville, TN)

Jonathan Jones, Casa de Proyecto Libertad Immigrant-Refugee Advocates, San Benito, TX

Marietta Jaeger Lane, Michigan Coalition for Human Rights Acting Director, Detroit, MI (now in Three Forks, MT)

Joan Lester, Equity Institute Executive Director, Berkeley, CA (now a writer/cultural worker, Berkeley, CA)

Jan Montgomery, Chronic Fatigue Immune Dysfunction Syndrome Association, Kailua, HI

Tema Okun, Grassroots Leadership Training Director, Charlotte, NC (now a non-profit consultant, Durham, NC)

Rev. David Ostendorf, PrairieFire Rural Action Executive Director, Des Moines, IA (now with Center for New Community, Ellsworth, WI)

Roz Ostendorf, Iowa Inter-Church Agency for Peace and Justice, Des Moines, IA (now with Center for New Community, Ellsworth, WI)

Michael Picker, National Toxics Campaign Fund West Coast Director, Sacramento, CA (now with Lincoln Crow Strategic Communications, Sacramento, CA)

Lee Pliscou, California Rural Legal Assistance, Loma Rica, CA

Jeffrey Richardson, Jobs With Peace Executive Director, Pittsburgh, PA (now in Los Angeles, CA)

Nancy Russell, North of Market Planning Coalition Executive Director, San Francisco, CA

Mab Segrest, North Carolinians Against Racist and Religious Violence, Durham, NC (now with Connecticut College, Gender and Women's Studies, New London, CT)

Jean (Idell) Smalls, Sea Island Youth Development Executive Director, Hollywood, SC)

Felicia Ward, Bay Area Black Women's Health Project Executive Director, Oakland, CA (now with New College of California Writing and Consciousness Program, San Francisco, CA)

1992

Carl Anthony, Urban Habitat Program Executive Director, San Francisco, CA (now with Ford Foundation, New York, NY)

Linda Burnham, Women of Color Resource Center, Oakland, CA

Sharon Delugach, Jobs With Peace, Los Angeles, CA (now with Office of Mayor Antonio Villaraigosa, Los Angeles, CA)

Julia Devin, International Commission on Medical Neutrality, Seattle, WA (now with International Rescue Committee, Seattle, WA)

Bob Fulkerson, Citizen Alert Executive Director, Reno, NV (now with Progressive Leadership Alliance of Nevada, Reno, NV)

Ronnie Gilbert, artist/cultural worker, Berkeley, CA

Cathy Howell, Grassroots Leadership Organizing Director, Charlotte, NC (now with National Organizers Alliance, Wilmington, NC)

Donna Land Maldonado, KRCL Community Radio, Salt Lake City, UT

Kamau Marcharia, Grassroots Leadership, Jenkinsville, SC

Terry Messman, American Friends Service Committee/Street Spirit, Oakland, CA

Maureen O'Connell, Save Our Cumberland Mountains, Lake City, TN

David Orr, Cook County Clerk's Office, Chicago, IL

Hank Perlin, Low-Income Housing Preservation, New York, NY (now with Department of Housing Preservation, New York, NY)

Bruce Plenk, Utah Legal Services Senior Attorney, Salt Lake City, UT (now in Tucson, AZ)

Linda Stout, Piedmont Peace Project Executive Director, Kannapolis, NC (now with Spirit in Action, Belchertown, MA)

Pnina Tobin, Children's Self-Help Center Executive Director, Oakland, CA (now with PMT Consultants, Berkeley, CA)

Arturo Vargas, Mexican-American Legal Defense and Educational Fund, Los Angeles, CA (now with National Association of Latino Elected Officials, Los Angeles, CA)

Judy Wanamaker, Appalachian Women's Guild, Sequatchie, TN

Marcy Whitebook, Center for the Child Care Work Force, Berkeley, CA (now with Center for the Study of Child Care Employment, Berkeley, CA)

Carol Prejean Zippert, WACC: Institute for Human Development Executive Director, Eutaw, AL (now with Society of Folk Arts and Culture, Eutaw, AL)

1993

Lois Jewel Barber, EarthAction, Amherst, MA

Louise Bauschard, Hyde Park Alliance Executive Director, St. Louis, MO (now with Community Corrections, Hillsboro, OR)

Ken Butigan, Pace e Bene Nonviolence Service, Chicago, IL

Gary Cohen, National Toxics Campaign Fund Executive Director, Boston, MA (now with Environmental Health Fund, Jamaica Plain, MA)

Nancy Davis, Equal Rights Advocates Executive Director, San Francisco, CA (now with San Francisco Trial Court, San Francisco, CA)

Joyce Dukes, Highlander Research and Education Center, New Market, TN (now with Commission on Religion in Appalachia, Knoxville, TN)

Katie Elliott-McCrea, Santa Cruz Westside Community Health Center Executive Director, Soquel, CA)

David Fair, We the People Living with AIDS/HIV of the Delaware Valley, Philadelphia, PA

Michael Fontana, Greater Cincinnati Coalition for the Homeless Executive Director, Cincinnati, OH

Octavia Hudson, Buffalo, NY

Suzanne Jones, Single Parent Resource Center, Inc., New York, NY

Terry Keleher, Kentuckians for the Commonwealth Organizer, London, KY (now with Applied Research Center, Chicago, IL)

Jackie Kittrell, American Environmental Health Studies Project, Knoxville, TN

Joyce Klemperer, Coalition of Battered Women's Advocates, New York, NY

Joseph Lam, Chinatown Youth Center Executive Director, San Francisco, CA

Jackie Lynn, Chicago Area Project Special Projects Director, Chicago, IL (now with Episcopal Peace Fellowship, Chicago, IL)

Marcy May, Effective Alternatives in Reconciliation Services, Bronx, NY

Dorris Pickens (deceased), The Neighborhood Institute, Chicago, IL

Sara Rios, Center for Constitutional Rights Attorney, New York, NY (now with Ford Foundation, New York, NY)

Berta "Bert" Saavedra, Los Angeles Alliance for a Drug-Free Community, Los Angeles, CA (now with Pico Union Family Resource Center, Baldwin Park, CA)

Professor Judith A. M. Scully, public interest attorney, Chicago, IL (now with West Virginia University Law School, Morgantown, WV)

Barbara Smith, Kitchen Table: Women of Color Press, Albany, NY

Jonathan Stein, Community Legal Services, Philadelphia, PA

Gwendolyn Johnson Winfree, Imani Business Service, Philadelphia, PA

1994

Alfreda Barringer, Grassroots Leadership, Charlotte, NC

Frances Hyde Crowe, Massachusetts American Friends Service Committee, Northampton, MA (now with Traprock Peace Center, Northampton, MA)

Mary Dailey, Northwest Bronx Community and Clergy Coalition Executive Director, Yonkers, NY (now with Center for Community Change, Yonkers, NY)

Nancy Dorsinville, Haitian American Women's Advocacy Network, New York, NY (now with Harvard Center for Population and Development Studies, Cambridge, MA)

Tonya Gonnella Frichner, American Indian Law Alliance, New York, NY

Emily Goldfarb, Northern California Coalition for Immigrant and Refugee Rights Executive Director, San Francisco, CA (now a nonprofit consultant, San Francisco, CA)

Delia Gomez, Las Americas Refugee Asylum Project Executive Director, El Paso, TX (now with The Women's Intercultural Center, Anthony, NM)

Running Grass, environmental justice consultant, Sausalito, CA

Deeanna L. Jang, Legal Assistance Foundation Staff Attorney, Oakland, CA (now with Office of Civil Rights, U.S. Department of Health and Human Services, Washington, DC)

Sandra Jerabek, Californians Against Waste Executive Director, Sacramento, CA (now with Friends of Del Norte and Redwood Economic Development Institute, Crescent City, CA)

Louis Jones, Standup Harlem Inc., New York, NY (now with Voices of Community Advocates and Leaders/New York Users Union, Brooklyn, NY)

Rev. Mac Charles Jones (deceased), Center for Democratic Renewal, Kansas City, KS

Beckie Masaki, Asian Women's Shelter, San Francisco, CA

Terry McGovern, HIV Law Project, New York, NY (now with Columbia University School of Public Health, New York, NY)

Jah'shams Abdul Mu'Min, Al Wooten Jr. Heritage Center Executive Director, Los Angeles, CA (now with Success: A New Beginning, Los Angeles, CA)

Bruce Occena, Acceptance Place/Baker Places Clinical Supervisor, Oakland, CA

Julie Quiroz-Martinez, National Immigration Forum, Washington, DC (now with mosaic consulting, Oakland, CA)

Luz Rodriguez, Washington Heights Ecumenical Food Pantry Executive Director, New York, NY (now with National School and Community Corps, Woodrow Wilson National Fellowship Foundation, Princeton, NJ)

Karen J. Stults, YouthAction Executive Director, Washington, DC)

Kay Whitlock, American Friends Service Committee, Des Moines, IA (now with American Friends Service Committee, Missoula, MT)

Susan Williams, Highlander Research and Education Center, New Market, TN

John Zippert, Federation of Southern Cooperatives, Eutaw, AL

1995

Kaleema Sumareh Biteye (Anne Sanders), United Community Housing Coalition, Detroit, MI

Sandra Camacho (deceased), La Casa de Las Madres, New York, NY

Ben Clarke, Tenderloin Reflection and Education Center, San Francisco, CA (now with Urban Habitat, Oakland, CA)

Luz de Leon, Philippine Resource Center, Daly City, CA

Tom di Maria, International Gay and Lesbian Human Rights Commission, San Francisco, CA

Susan Freundlich, Redwood Cultural Work Director, Oakland, CA (now with Women's Foundation of California, Oakland, CA)

Bill Gallegos, Los Angeles Alliance for a Drug-Free Community, Los Angeles, CA (now with Communities for a Better Environment, Huntington Park, CA)

Vickie Goodwin, Powder River Basin Resource Council, Sheridan, WY

David Grant, Rural Southern Voice for Peace, St. Louis, MO (now with International Fellowship of Reconciliation, the Netherlands)

Eric Mann, Labor/Community Strategy Center, Los Angeles, CA

Laurin Mayeno, Community Health Academy, Berkeley, CA

Kim McClain, Citizen's Research Education Network, Hartford, CT (now with Community Associations Institute–CT Chapter, Hartford, CT

Mary McColl, Planned Parenthood of Idaho, Boise, ID

Ellen Moore, Adolescent HIV Services Coordinator at San Francisco General Hospital, San Francisco, CA (now in graduate school)

LeRoy Moore, Rocky Mountain Peace and Justice Center, Boulder, CO

Rondy Murray, Clerical-Technical Union of Michigan State University Organizer, Lansing, MI (now with Michigan Education Association, Lansing, MI)

Cate Poe, ACORN Education Reform Director, Brooklyn, NY (now a nonprofit consultant, Brooklyn, NY)

Holly Pruett, Oregon Coalition Against Domestic and Sexual Violence, Portland, OR

Linda Waters Richardson, Black United Fund of Pennsylvania, Philadelphia, PA

Gloria Simoneaux, Drawbridge Arts Program for Homeless Children, San Rafael, CA

Tim Smith, Interfaith Center on Corporate Responsibility, New York, NY (now with Walden Asset Management, Boston, MA)

Michael Stoops, National Coalition for the Homeless, Washington, DC

Barbara Hanson Treen, WOMEN Care, Inc. Executive Director, New York, NY (now with The Restorative Justice Project, Ogunquit, ME)

Geraldine Zapata, Plaza Community Center, Los Angeles, CA

1996

Nancy Ailes, Pine Cabin Run Ecological Laboratory, High View, WV

Maria Blanco, Women's Employment Rights Clinic at Golden Gate University School of Law, San Francisco, CA (now with Lawyers Committee for Civil Rights, San Francisco, CA)

Robert Bray, National Gay and Lesbian Task Force, Washington, DC (now with Public Interest Projects, San Francisco, CA and New York, NY)

Leslie Cagan, Cuba Information Project Executive Director, New York, NY (now with United for Peace and Justice, Elmhurst, NY)

Francis Calpotura, Center for Third World Organizing Co-Director, Oakland, CA (now with Transnational Institute for Grassroots Research and Action, Oakland, CA)

Pamela Costain, Resource Center of the Americas, Minneapolis, MN (now with Wellstone Action, St. Paul, MN)

Stefano DeZerega, Overseas Development Network Executive Director, San Francisco, CA (now a public school teacher, San Francisco, CA)

Audrey Evans, Tulane Environmental Clinic, New Orleans, LA

buddy gray (deceased), Drop Inn Center, Cincinnati, OH

Freddie Hamilton, Child Development Support Corporation, Brooklyn, NY

M. Gloria Hernandez, California Rural Legal Assistance Migrant Farmworker Project, Fresno, CA (now with Comite No Nos Vamos, Fresno, CA)

Karen Lehman, Institute for Agriculture and Trade Policy, Minneapolis, MN (now with The Minnesota Project, St. Paul, MN)

Steve Lew, Living Well Project, San Francisco, CA (now with CompassPoint, San Francisco, CA)

Miriam Ching Louie, Asian Immigrant Women Advocates Media and Research Coordinator, Oakland, CA (now a writer, Oakland, CA)

Cindy Marano (deceased), Wider Opportunities for Women Executive Director, Oakland, CA

Joan McCracken, InterMountain Planned Parenthood Director, Billings, MT

Juana Alicia Montoya, East Bay Institute for Urban Arts Co-Director, Oakland, CA (now an artist/cultural worker, Berkeley, CA)

Daniel Nicolai, Lousiana Labor-Neighbor Project Executive Director, Baton Rouge, LA (now with Service Employees International Union (SEIU) Justice for Janitors, Boston, MA)

Thomas Quinn, Wisconsin Farmland Conservancy, Menomonie, WI

Raul Salinas, Resistencia Bookstore and Red Salmon Press, Austin, TX

Jane Sapp, Center for Cultural and Community Development, Springfield, MA

Gail Smith, Chicago Legal Aid to Incarcerated Mothers, Chicago, IL

Phyllis Taylor, peace worker, Philadelphia, PA

Richard Taylor, peace worker, Philadelphia, PA

Jill Tregor, Intergroup Clearinghouse, San Francisco, CA (now a consultant to grassroots organizations, Oakland, CA)

Larry Weiss, Resource Center of the Americas, Minneapolis, MN

1997

Fran Barrett, Community Resource Exchange, New York, NY

Betsy Barton, North Carolina Occupational Safety and Health Project, Durham, NC

Diane T. Chin, Office of Citizen Complaints of the City of San Francisco, San Francisco, CA (now with Office of Career Services, Stanford Law School, Stanford, CA)

Julie Dorf, International Gay and Lesbian Human Rights Commission Executive Director, San Francisco, CA (now with Horizons Foundation, San Francisco, CA)

Rev. Richard Estrada, CMF, Jovenes, Inc., Los Angeles, CA

Thomas Patrick Fenton, Bulletin of Concerned Asian Scholars, Cedar, MI

Brad Fields, Maryland Food Committee, Columbia, MD

Jennifer L. Gordon, Workplace Project Executive Director, Hempstead, NY (now with Fordham Law School, Brooklyn, NY)

Jennifer Grant, Riley Center: Services for Battered Women and Their Children, San Francisco, CA

LeeAnn Hall, Northwest Federation of Community Organizations, Seattle, WA

Erica Harrold, California Peace Action, Oakland, CA

Timothea "Tim" Howard, Columbia Heights/Shaw Family Support Collaborative Lead Organizer, Washington, DC

Teresa Ying Hsu, Asian-American Communications, New York, NY

Madeline Janis-Aparicio, Los Angeles Alliance for a New Economy, Los Angeles, CA

Richard Juarez, Metropolitan Area Advisory Committee, San Diego, CA (now with Urban West Development Consultants, Bonita, CA)

Theresa M. Keaveny, Dakota Rural Action Organizer, Brookings, SD (now with Montana Conservation Voters, Billings, MT)

Oren Lyons, Center for the Americas, SUNY Buffalo, Buffalo, NY

David Mann, Minnesota Alliance for Progressive Action Co-Director, St. Paul. MN (now consultant to grassroots organizations, Minneapolis, MN)

David Mendoza, National Campaign for Freedom of Expression, Seattle, WA

David K. Miller, International Union of Operating Engineers, Charlotte, NC (now in Placitas, NM)

Rev. Jim Mitulski, Metropolitan Community Church Pastor, San Francisco, CA (now with Metropolitan Community Churches, Los Angeles, CA)

Millard "Mitty" Owens, Center for Community Self-Help, Durham, NC (now with New York University, New York, NY)

Jackie Workman, National Council of Churches, Blair, SC

1998

Olga Morales Aguirre (deceased), The Mujeres Project, San Antonio, TX

Alexa Bradley, Minnesota Alliance for Progressive Action Co-Director, St. Paul, MN (now with Grassroots Policy Project, Milwaukee, WI)

Gene Bruskin, Food and Allied Services Trades, AFL-CIO, Washington, DC

Estelle Chun, Asian Pacific American Legal Center, Los Angeles, CA

Walter Davis, Southern Empowerment Project, Maryville, TN

Bill Fields, Under One Sky, Seymour, TN

Kathleen Geathers, Greater Cleveland Coalition for A Clean Environment, Cleveland, OH

Pat Gowens, Welfare Warriors, Milwaukee, WI

Mel Grizer, United Community Centers, Inc., Brooklyn, NY

Eileen Hansen, AIDS Legal Referral Panel, San Francisco, CA

Pharis Harvey, International Labor Rights Fund, Washington, DC

Cristina Jose-Kampfner, National Center for Women in Prison, Ann Arbor, MI

Jereann King, Literacy South, Warrenton, NC

Linda Price King, Environmental Health Network, Chesapeake, VA

Barbara Miner, Rethinking Schools, Milwaukee, WI

Charlene Mitchell, Committees of Correspondence, New York, NY

Barbara Moore (deceased), Charlotte Organizing Project, Charlotte, NC

Mary O'Brien, Citizens for Public Accountability, Eugene, OR

Mike Odom, The Center for Public Trust, Birmingham, AL (now with Legal Environmental Assistance Foundation, Tallahassee, FL)

Jose Orta, Austin Latino/a Lesbian and Gay Organization, Taylor, TX

Sonia Pena, Center for Third World Organizing, Denver, CO (now with Applied Research Center, Oakland, CA)

Michael Prokosch, Committee in Solidarity with the People of El Salvador, Boston, MA (now with the Labor Extension Program–University of Massachusetts, Dorchester, MA)

Debra Rubin, Women's Law Project, Philadelphia, PA

Joel Shufro, NY Committee for Occupational Safety and Health (NYCOSH), New York, NY

Gladis Sibrian, Centro Latino Cuzcatlan Organizer, San Francisco, CA

Beulah White, Five Rivers Community Development Corporation, Georgetown, SC

1999

Stuart Acuff, Atlanta Central Labor Council Executive Director, Atlanta, GA (now with AFL-CIO Organizing Department, Washington, DC)

Adrienne Anderson, University of Colorado at Boulder, Denver, CO

Mandy Carter, National Black Lesbian and Gay Leadership Forum, Durham, NC (now a consultant to grassroots organizations, Durham, NC)

Brenda Cummings, Women's Health Rights Coalition, Oakland, CA

Diane D'Arrigo, Nuclear Information and Resource Services, Washington, DC

Laura Gordon, Western NC Central Labor Council/Teamsters Local 61, Marshall, NC

Marge Grevatt, Center for Cooperative Action Executive Director, Cleveland Heights, OH

Pronita Gupta, Los Angeles Alliance for a New Economy, Los Angeles, CA (now with Asian Americans Pacific Islanders in Philanthropy, San Francisco, CA)

Lisa Hoyos, Working Partnerships, San Jose, CA (now with Public Citizen, Oakland, CA)

Joshua Hoyt, United Power for Action and Justice Organizer, Chicago, IL (now Director of Illinois Coalition for Immigrant and Refugee Rights, Chicago, IL)

Virginia Rodriguez Jones, Communication Workers of America AFL-CIO, Oakland, CA

Lani Ka'ahumanu, BiNet USA, BiPOL, National Gay and Lesbian Task Force, San Francisco, CA

Helen Sunhee Kim, Asian Immigrant Women Advocates Organizer, San Jose, CA (now a consultant to grassroots organizations, Oakland, CA)

Richard Kirsch, Citizen Action of New York, Albany, NY

Eric Mar, Northern California Coalition for Immigrant Rights Executive Director, San Francisco, CA (now on San Francisco Board of Education, San Francisco, CA)

Jacqueline Nia Mason, Action for Community Empowerment Executive Director, New York, NY

Clayton McCracken, MD, InterMountain Planned Parenthood, Billings, MT

Peggy Saika, Asian Pacific Environmental Network Executive Director, Oakland, CA (now with Asian Americans Pacific Islanders in Philanthropy, San Francisco, CA)

Jim Sessions, Highlander Research and Education Center Executive Director, New Market, TN (now with Jobs with Justice, Knoxville, TN)

Michael James Shay, South Arundel Citizens for Responsible Development, Churchton, MD

Jessica Govea Thorbourne (deceased), Industrial and Labor Relations School of Cornell University, West Orange, NJ

Fran Tobin, Rogers Park Community Action Network Executive Director, Chicago, IL

Andrea van den Heever, Connecticut Center for New Economy, New Haven, CT

Eric Ward, Northwest Coalition for Human Dignity Executive Director, Seattle, WA (now with Center for New Community, Chicago, IL)

Leah Wise, Southeastern Regional Economic Justice Network, Durham, NC

Diane Wood, New Mexico Coalition of Labor Union Women, New Mexico Women's Foundation, Albuquerque, NM

Beth Zilbert, Calcasieu League for Environmental Action Now Organizer, Lake Charles, LA

2000

Jane Alexander, Women's Lunch Place, Boston, MA

Cassandra Allen, UNITE/HERE, Washington, DC

Leon Allen, UNITE/HERE, Washington, DC

Ronald Aubourg, Haitian Centers Council, Brooklyn, NY

Jeff Bartow, Interfaith Leadership Project, Cicero, IL (now with Southwest Organizing Project, Chicago, IL)

Mary Burns, The Maura Clarke–Ita Ford Center, Richmond Hill, NY

Pamela Chiang, Asian Pacific Environmental Network Organizer, Oakland, CA (now with Center for Community Change, Belgrade, MT)

Martha Davis, NOW Legal Defense and Education Fund, New York, NY

Trishala Deb, The Audre Lorde Project, Brooklyn, NY

Donna Dudley, New Life Women's Leadership Project, Willamston, NC

Steve Fendt, Southside Organizing Committee, Milwaukee, WI

Lora Jo Foo, Asian Law Caucus Staff Attorney, San Francisco, CA (now with California Faculty Association, Castro Valley, CA)

P. Catlin Fullwood, On Time Associates Consulting, Chicago, IL

Kathy Goldman, Community Food Resource Center Executive Director, New York, NY

Simon Greer, Jobs With Justice in Washington, DC, (now with Jewish Funds for Justice, New York, NY)

Ann Pickel Harris, We the People Inc. Tennessee, Rockwood, TN

Dan Hirsch, Committee to Bridge the Gap, Santa Cruz, CA

Anthony "Van" Jones, Ella Baker Center for Human Rights, Oakland, CA

Burt Lauderdale, Kentuckians for the Commonwealth, London, KY

Enid Lee, National Coalition of Education Activists, Santa Cruz, CA

David Mann, Peninsula Interfaith Action, San Jose, CA

Adriana Portillo-Bartow, Greater Lawn Community Youth Network, Chicago, IL (now with Where Are the Children Project, Chicago, IL)

Phyllis Salowe-Kaye, New Jersey Citizen Action, West Orange, NJ

Rinku Sen, Center for Third World Organizing Co-Director, Oakland, CA (now with Applied Research Center, New York, NY)

Triana Silton, Service Employees International Union (SEIU), Los Angeles, CA

Esmeralda Simmons, Center for Law and Social Justice, Brooklyn, NY

Bill Smedley, AIR / PEN / Greenwatch, Jersey Shore, PA

Vicki Smedley, AIR / PEN / Greenwatch, Jersey Shore, PA

Sharon Streater, Hillsborough Organization for Progress and Equality (HOPE), Tampa, FL)

2001

Jan Adams, Applied Research Center Associate Director, Oakland, CA (now a consultant to grassroots organizations, San Francisco, CA)

Dothula Baron-Hall, The Dispute Settlement Center Executive Director, Warsaw, NC)

Dennis Bernstein, KPFA / Pacifica Radio, Berkeley, CA

Regina Botterill, Interfaith Worker Justice, Chicago, IL

Vivian Chang, Environmental and Economic Justice Project Organizer, Los Angeles, CA (now with Asian Pacific Environmental Network, Oakland, CA)

Scott Douglas, Greater Birmingham Ministries, Birmingham, AL

Stephanie Gut, San Diego Organizing Project, San Diego, CA

Gilda Haas, Strategic Actions for a Just Economy, Los Angeles, CA

Jerry Hardt, Kentuckians for the Commonwealth, Salyersville, KY

Christopher Ho, Employment Law Center, San Francisco, CA

Robert J. Hudek, Wisconsin Citizen Action, Madison, WI

Taj James, Movement Strategy Center, Oakland, CA

Vernon Damani Johnson, Northwest Coalition for Human Dignity, Bellingham, WA

Lana Landaverde, SHARE Foundation, Daly City, CA

Denny Larsen, Communities for a Better Environment, San Francisco, CA (now with Global Community Monitor, San Francisco, CA)

Jacquie Leavy, Neighborhood Capital Budget Group, Oak Park, IL

Ruby Mouton, Louisiana Injured Workers Union, Terrytown, LA

Torm Nompraseurt, Laotian Organizing Project/Asian Pacific Environmental Network, Richmond, CA

Juliana Perez, PATCH and MATCH Programs for Incarcerated Parents, San Antonio, TX

Joy Persall, Headwaters Fund Program Director, Minneapolis, MN (now with Native Americans in Philanthropy, Minneapolis, MN)

Janis Plotkin, Jewish Film Festival Executive Director, Oakland, CA

Anne Rabe, Citizens Environmental Coalition Executive Director, Castleton, NY

Rosi Reyes, Applied Research Center, Oakland, CA (now with SPIN Project, San Francisco, CA)

Janet Robideau, Montana People's Action, Missoula, MT

Don Stahlhut, Contra Costa Interfaith Sponsoring Committee (CCISCO), Martinez, CA

Tanya Tull, Beyond Shelter, Los Angeles, CA

Angeles Valverde, Hotel Workers Union rank and file activist, Los Angeles, CA (now with Service Employees International Union (SEIU) Local 434B, Los Angeles, CA)

2002

Barbara Ayotte, Physicians for Human Rights, Concord, MA

Dianne Bady, Ohio Valley Environmental Coalition, Proctorville, OH

Allen Bernard, Louisiana Injured Workers Union, New Orleans, LA

Michaelann Bewsee, Arise for Social Justice, Springfield, MA

Miriam Brown, OP, Churches' Center for Land and People, Milwaukee, WI

Devin Burghart, Center for New Community, Chicago, IL

Steve Cagan, Cleveland Jobs With Justice, Cleveland Heights, OH

Pat Clifford, Drop Inn Center, Cincinnati, OH

Donald Cohen, Center on Policy Initiatives, San Diego, CA

Rev. John Heinemeier, Greater Boston Interfaith Organization, Boston, MA (now with BUILD, Baltimore, MD)

Katy Heins, Contact Center, Cincinnati, OH

Tula Jaffe, Labor and Social Action Summer School/ Service Employees International Union (SEIU), Local 707, Sebastopol, CA

Jose Matus, Derechos Humanos/Alianza Indigena, Tucson, AZ

Tonya McClary, American Friends Service Committee, Philadelphia, PA

John McDermott, Lakeview Action Coalition Executive Director, Chicago, IL (now with Logan Square Neighborhood Association, Chicago, IL)

Blanca Moreno, Farmworkers Association of Florida, Apopka, FL

Tirso Moreno, Farmworkers Association of Florida, Apopka, FL

John Musick, Michigan Organizing Project, Muskegon, MI

Karen Narasaki, Asian American Justice Center, Washington, DC

Jeanne Otersen, Health Professionals and Allied Employees/AFT/AFL-CIO, Emerson, NJ)

Donna Parson, Public Campaign, Washington, DC (now with Demos, New York, NY)

Deepak Pateriya, SCOPE/AGENDA Organizer, Los Angeles, CA (now with Service Employees International Union (SEIU) Local 1877, San Francisco, CA)

Rosalyn (Roz) Pelles, Union Community Fund, Silver Spring, MD

Frances Reid, Iris Films, Oakland, CA

Graciela Sanchez, Esperanza Peace and Justice Center, San Antonio, TX

Denise Scheer, Michigan Organizing Project, Muskegon, MI

Naomi Swinton, Grassroots Leadership, Wilmington, NC

Pamela Twiss, ISAIAH Co-Director, Minneapolis, MN (now with Service Employees International Union (SEIU), Local 284, Minneapolis, MN)

Leonardo Vilchis, Union de Vecinos, Los Angeles, CA

Cindy Wiesner, People Organized to Win Employment Rights (POWER) Organizer, San Francisco, CA (now with Miami Workers Center, Miami, FL)

Sherry Williams, Treasure Island Homeless Development Initiative, San Francisco, CA

Susan Alva, Coalition for Humane Immigrant Rights of Los Angeles, Los Angeles, CA (now with Migration Policy and Resource Center, Los Angeles, CA)

Nikki Fortunato Bas, Sweatshop Watch Executive Director, Oakland, CA

Beverley Bell, Center for Economic Justice, Albuquerque, NM

Jennifer Blevins, Jobs and Affordable Housing Campaign–FCS, Minneapolis, MN

Les Brown, Chicago Coalition for the Homeless, Chicago, IL

Jim Cook, Service Employees International Union (SEIU) Local 503, Salem, OR

Rick Engler, Work Environment Council of New Jersey, Moorestown, NJ

Holly Fincke, Just Cause Oakland, Oakland, CA (now Director of Windcall, Oakland, CA)

Susan R. Gordon, Alliance for Nuclear Accountability, Seattle, WA

Elena M. Herrada, Committee for the Political Resurrection of Detroit, Detroit, MI

Rachel Jackson, Books Not Bars, Ella Baker Center for Human Rights, San Francisco, CA

Lucy Lewis, Greensboro Justice Fund, Carrboro, NC

Ted Lewis, Global Exchange, San Francisco, CA

Larry Lipschultz, Health Professionals and Allied Employees/AFT/AFL-CIO, Emerson, NJ

Pamela Miller, Alaska Community Action on Toxics, Anchorage, AK

Jose Montenegro, International Center for Sustainable Rural Development (CIDERS), Salinas, CA

Stephanie Wilson Moore, Fannie Lou Hamer Project, Kalamazoo, MI

Clara Luz Navarro, Mujeres Unidas y Activas, New America Foundation, San Francisco, CA

Betty Robinson, Citizen's Planning and Housing Association, Baltimore, MD

Judy Robinson, Environmental Health Fund, Jamaica Plain, MA

Melissa Spatz, Blocks Together Co-Director, Chicago, IL (now with Women and Girls' Leadership Project c/o ICAH, Chicago, IL)

Miriam Thompson, Office of Worker Education, Queens College, Flushing, NY

Consuelo Valdez, Proyecto Pastoral at Dolores Mission, Los Angeles, CA

Mildred Wiley, Bethel New Life, Chicago, IL

Beulah White, Five Rivers Community Development Corp., Georgetown, SC

Donna Wong, Hawaii's Thousand Friends, Kailua, HI

2004

Rebecca Bauen, Women's Action to Gain Economic Security Executive Director, Oakland, CA (now with Mayfair Improvement Initiative, San Jose, CA)

Ilana Berger, Families United for Racial and Economic Equality, Brooklyn, NY

Susan Burton, A New Way of Life, Los Angeles, CA

Margi Clarke, consultant to grassroots organizations, Berkeley, CA

Kirsten Cross, East Bay Alliance for a Sustainable Economy, Oakland, CA (now with INFACT, Oakland, CA)

Sharon M. Day, Indigenous Peoples Task Force, St. Paul, MN

Grace M. Dickerson, For Love of Children, Washington, DC

Jim Dickerson, MANNA, Inc. and New Community Church, Washington, DC

Conny Ford, San Francisco Labor Council and OPEIU Local 3, Daly City, CA

Lenny Foster, Navajo Nation Corrections Project, Window Rock, AZ

Janet Fout, Ohio Valley Environmental Coalition, Huntington, WV

Neris Amanda Gonzalez, Ecovida, Chicago, IL

Winnett W. Hagens, Democracy South, Virginia Beach, VA

Jaribu Hill, Mississippi Workers' Center for Human Rights, Greenville, MS

Sibal Holt, Louisiana State AFL-CIO, Baton Rouge, LA

Stacy Kono, Asian Immigrant Women Advocates, Berkeley, CA

Lynn MacMichael, Voices in the Wilderness/Fellowship of Reconciliation, Lafayette, CA

Rev. Terry Allen Moe, Metro Alliance for Common Good and Redeemer Lutheran, Portland, OR

Kirsten Irgens Moller, Global Exchange, San Francisco, CA

Ruben Nunez, Colonias Development Council, Las Cruces, NM

Roberta Perry, National Farmworkers Ministry, DeLand, FL

Suzanne Pharr, Highlander Research and Education Center Executive Director, New Market, TN (now a nonprofit consultant, Knoxville, TN)

Alex Poeter, Brighton Park Neighborhood Council, Chicago, IL

Bill Ravanesi, Health Care Without Harm, Longmeadow, MA

Nina Shapiro-Perl, Service Employees International Union (SEIU), Silver Spring, MD

Roger Sherman, United Vision for Idaho, Boise, ID

Steve Taylor, Military Toxics Project, Portland, ME (now with Environmental Health Strategy Center, Portland, ME)

Alan Watahara, The Watahara Group, Sacramento, CA

Melinda Wiggins, Student Action with Farmworkers, Durham, NC

Sister Margaret Zalot, SSC, Southwest Organizing Project and Maria High School, Chicago, IL

2005

Pam Baldwin, The Interfaith Alliance of Idaho, Meridian, ID

Elsa Barboza, SCOPE/AGENDA, Los Angeles, CA

Rev. Carrie Bolton, Democracy South/Alston Chapel United Holy Church, Pittsboro, NC

Susan Braine, Koahnic Broadcast Corporation, Albuquerque, NM

Cheryl Brown, Labor Project for Working Families, Oakland, CA (now with Contra Costa County Labor Council, Oakland, CA)

Joannie C. Chang, Asian Law Caucus, San Francisco, CA

Richard Deats, Fellowship of Reconciliation, Nyack, NY

Lisa Duran, Derechos Para Todos/Rights for All People, Denver, CO

P. Catlin Fullwood, On Time Associates Consulting, Chicago, IL

Arnie Graf, Industrial Areas Foundation, Ellicott City, MD

Marielena Hincapie, National Immigration Law Center, Los Angeles, CA

Liz Jacobs, California Nurses Association, Oakland, CA

Michael Johnston, Teamsters Local 890, Watsonville, CA

Scott Kennedy, Resource Center for Nonviolence, Santa Cruz, CA

Debora Kodish, Philadelphia Folklore Project, Philadelphia, PA

Karen Jo Koonan, National Lawyer's Guild/National Jury Project, San Francisco, CA

Mary Lassen, The Women's Union Executive Director, Dorchester, MA

Kay Matthews, La Jicarita News, Chamisal, NM

Mary Ochs, Center for Community Change Lead Organizer, Downey, CA

Jack Payden-Travers, Virginians Against the Death Penalty, Charlottesville, VA

Maria Poblet, St. Peter's Housing Committee, San Francisco, CA

Rev. John Powis, Bushwick Housing Independence Project and St. Barbara's R.C. Church, New York, NY

Eric Quezada, Mission Anti-displacement Coalition, San Francisco, CA (now with Dolores Street Community Services, San Francisco, CA)

Andy Robinson, consultant to grassroots organizations, Plainfield, VT

Hector Rodriguez, Proyecto Esperanza, Columbia, MD

Roger Sherman, United Vision for Idaho, Boise, ID

Diana Spatz, LIFETIME, Oakland, CA

Vivian Stockman, Ohio Valley Environmental Coalition, Spencer, WV

Ann Twomey, Health Professionals and Allied Employees/AFT/AFL-CIO, Rutherford, NJ

Loretta Vaughn, Harriet Tubman–Fannie Lou Hamer Collective, Springfield Gardens, NY

About the Author and Contributors

Susan Wells has been active in the social justice movement since the 1950s, often pushing one of her three children in a stroller to attend a local demonstration or rally. She and her husband, Albert, are founding board members of the Abelard Foundation, which has been supporting social change efforts since the civil rights movement.

In the late sixties, Susan pursued a long-held interest in psychology by helping to create and staff a nonprofit, low-cost counseling center in Palo Alto, California. She subsequently returned to school for a graduate degree and, at forty-one, opened a private practice in adult psychotherapy.

In 1986, envisioning a peaceful summer home in the mountains, Susan and Albert purchased a stunning half-section of land on the lower slopes of the Bridger Range in Montana. But their desire to remain involved in the social justice movement soon had them exploring ways to share the land with others. In the fall of 1989 they opened a residential program to address the frequent incidence of leadership burnout in social change organizations.

Susan and Albert ran the Windcall Resident Program four months of each year for sixteen years, hosting over four hundred social change organizers and activists from all over the United States. Today, the couple splits their time between Montana and a home in Northern California. In addition to their three adult children they have four grandchildren ranging in age from twenty-one to ten.

Sally Lehrman, an independent journalist, specializes in covering identity, race relations and gender within the context of science and medicine. She was a John S. Knight Fellow at Stanford University and is an Institute for Justice and Journalism Expert Fellow on race.

Lehrman is the author of *News in a New America,* a fresh take on diversity in media coverage and staffing, and serves as national diversity chair for the Society of Professional Journalists. Her work with The DNA Files, a series of radio documentaries distributed by National Public Radio, won a shared 2002 Peabody award, Peabody/Robert Wood Johnson Award for excellence in health and medical programming, and a Columbia/Du Pont Silver Baton. Lehrman works in her home office on the California coast with her assistant, Daisy, a St. Bernard.

George B. Wells has a master's degree in architecture and is a sculptor and photographer. In 2005 he traveled around the United States to meet and photograph the seven profiled Windcall residents. George lives in Healdsburg, California, with his wife, Shea.